DON'T JUST RETIRE
Live it, Love it!
a personal planning guide to enhance life after work

Written by
Richard Atkinson

Edited by
Mike Muxlow

© 2009   1060174

Text and illustrations copyright © 2009 by Retire Right Publications
Cartoon Illustrations copyright © www.cartoonstock.com

Published in Canada by Retire Right Publications
7 Blue Anchor Trail, Toronto, ON, Canada M1C 3N9
P. 416-282-7320 • F. 416-282-4260
ramgt@rogers.com • www.dontjustretire.com

Library and Archives Canada Cataloguing in Publication

Atkinson, Richard, 1941-
Don't just retire, *Live it! Love it!* : a personal planning guide to enhance life after work / written by Richard Atkinson ; edited by Mike Muxlow.

Includes bibliographical references and index.
ISBN 978-0-9811065-0-2

1. Retirement--Planning. 2. Retirement--Psychological aspects. I. Muxlow, Mike, 1972- II. Title.

HQ1062.A84 2009   646.7'9   C2008-906070-9

Designed by Altered Perception Inc.
Printed and bound in Canada by Friesens

Looking for a guest speaker?
Contact us at:
www.dontjustretire.com
(416) 282-7320

In memory of my Father,

John (Jack) Atkinson

- Remembered Forever -

ACKNOWLEDGEMENTS

The personal stories that appear in this book have been gathered over many years from a variety of sources – some of whom I can't remember because they have become part of my lifetime concern with retirement. Some stories came from retirees, and soon to become retirees. Other stories came from friends and acquaintances including fellow members of the Tam Heather Venerables Curling Club. The Venerables is Canada's largest senior's curling club.

My sincere gratitude to Dan Slovitt, Retired Journalist and Trevor Townsend of Richardson Partners Financial Limited, who not only encouraged the writing of this book but also helped edit my drafts. I will be forever in their debt!

I'd also like to thank Mike Muxlow of Muxlow Creative for his outstanding editing including his enhancement of my writing. Also for Mike's confidence, support and invaluable advice in making this book more reader friendly.

I thank my wife, Christine, for her patience and understanding, and my family for their encouragement and input.

FOREWORD

There is life after work, you just have to find it and make certain you do it right.

And to help make certain you're on the right path, Rick Atkinson has written Don't Just Retire - *Live It, Love It!* and in this book, it's not all about the money.

Just a month prior to my plunge into retirement, Rick told me about his book (unlike others who profess to be 'writing' a book, he had actually written it). Lo and behold, it opened my eyes to a myriad of topics that I hadn't even considered – the right time of the year to retire, making lists to keep me focused as the day went along, journaling to capture my thoughts and actions and ways to save money. And those are only a few of the topics - he does cover the money part of it, too!

After many decades in the news business where our products were fresh 24/7, I led a very busy urban lifestyle and found it difficult to slow down. The structure from Rick's book guided me into an understanding of how to better plan my time. And I found that I could on occasion simply say "to heck with the world; I'm going to do what I want today."

Rick saw what retirement did to a number of his colleagues and a close family member and wanted to make certain that he didn't fail in his retirement. And as an extremely organized human resources professional in his working life, he was certain that he had the structure to retire right.

Don't Just Retire – *Live It, Love It!* is for anyone contemplating retirement and the earlier one reads it the better to get on the right path towards retirement planning. Even if you're already in that wonderful phase of your life, guidance from the book can enhance the life you are leading, making certain you're getting the most out of your 'golden years.'

Dan Slovitt
Retired journalist and logistics manager

TABLE OF CONTENTS
DON'T JUST RETIRE – *LIVE IT, LOVE IT!*

INTRODUCTION

So you're thinking about retirement! Sitting at your desk or standing by your machine, you picture waking up in the morning when you're ready, lounging around the house with a cup of coffee and the paper, calling up friends for tennis or a game of golf and playing cards in the evening. Ah, freedom at last! You're no longer working. You're no longer commuting. For the first time in a long time, you're really enjoying life. Finally, you are retired!

When most people think about retirement, they imagine leaving a job they dislike, dropping out of the rat race and turning their back on the pressures of employment. They often see retirement as a welcome change or an escape to something more peaceful and serene.

But retiring is not only about giving up your job and relaxing. It's entering one of the most exciting and challenging stages of life. It can be a time to draw upon your personal and professional experiences to open new doors of opportunity and education. It can be the time when you realize your potential and accomplish significant goals previously delayed by the responsibilities of working and raising a family.

The opportunities in retirement are endless, however a successful retirement doesn't come without its hurdles. There are many considerations such as living on a reduced income, creating a health and wellness strategy, examining relationships with family and friends, allocating personal time, establishing living arrangements, adopting and adapting to different social roles and adjusting to the eventual death of a spouse, friends and family members.

Even though your retirement years should be a lifetime highlight, it can be a lot like a marshmallow. Soft and sweet in parts but also gooey to the point you get bogged down and are unable to move forward.

During the first days, weeks or maybe even months of retirement, there is often a blissful 'honeymoon' feeling. Life is wonderful! No more boss. No more job. No worries or cares. Just time to sit around and do whatever crosses your mind. During this period there is little motivation to plan for the future.

But as the honeymoon period winds down, a number of newly minted retirees report a feeling of disenchantment. Retirement no longer feels like an extended holiday. Time begins to weigh heavily on their shoulders. Playing golf five times a week begins to feel like a chore. Projects around the house lose their appeal and there is a 'let-down' kind of feeling that causes retirees to ask the question "Is this all there is?" Frustration and disappointment can mount as some retirees get caught in this vortex and are unable to get out.

In the quest for a successful retirement, you need to recognize its changing image. Retirement used to mean people were over-the-hill, sent out-to-pasture, or ready for the final sunset. In other words, retirees were starting the next chapter in life as non-productive, non-contributing members of society. Even today, many retirees have a pessimistic view of their non-working years. They see themselves already having made their contribution to their family and society and have mentally 'hung up their skates'. They do not expect much from retirement and unfortunately, that's just what they get.

The good news is a quiet revolution has been taking place regarding the image of retirement and the role of the retiree. Retired people and those about to retire are beginning to understand that there is a secret to a successful retirement. It is to be positive, stay actively involved and in control of their lives. Be an active participant in their neighborhoods, clubs and life in general. Today's retirees are becoming energized and are actively pursuing their life goals. By adopting vitality and a zest for living, they are electing to be enthusiastic about the future and are determined to shape their destinies as much as possible.

Successful retirees recognize the need to plan for happiness and productivity. They evaluate what's important to them and construct actions to satisfy their needs and wants. By creating a vision of a realistic retirement and building an action plan to achieve it, they are proactively and energetically seeking results.

So now, the choice is yours. Reserve your place in the rocking chair or grab the ring of life. Sit and wait for whatever comes along or tackle the challenges and opportunities. Be sedentary and without purpose or get involved and make a difference. Once again, the choice is yours.

This book is designed to assist with your retirement planning process. It outlines some of the problems and questions to be addressed when thinking about retirement and is intended to provide you with insight and direction, without taking away from your individual decision-making.

The inspiration for "Don't Just Retire - *Live It, Love It!*" came from observing people who retired from successful careers to lead inactive lives focused around television programs or computer games. Many had no hobbies or outside interests. Few had friends other than 'work buddies' and most were reluctant to join any organizations or social clubs. For some, they had relatively short lives after retiring and for others, they appeared unhappy and unfulfilled. Though tragic, it is not uncommon and I believe such unhappy endings can be prevented.

If you are around or between the ages of 45 to 65, it's time to explore your future as a retired person. Consider the contents of this book and take the time to complete the exercises. Be sure to share your thoughts and plans with your spouse or partner as you progress towards developing your personal retirement vision and plan.

Thank you for taking a proactive interest in your retirement and all the best in developing a plan that enriches your life.

Kindest regards,

Richard Atkinson

CHAPTER 1
YOUR RETIREMENT. YOUR DREAM.

You'll be happy to know that as you're planning your retirement, you are in good company.

 The 2006 Statistics Canada Census found those 65 years and older comprised 13% of Canada's population. By the year 2057, those aged 65 and older may reach 27%.

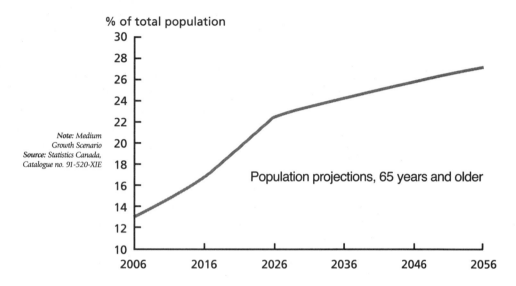

The same 2006 Census also determined the fastest growing age group between 2001 and 2006, was individuals aged 55 to 64. In fact, these nearly 3.7 million people represent an increase of 28.1% from 2001. This rate of growth is more than 5 times the national average of 5.4%.

Not surprisingly, longevity in Canada is also on the rise. In 2003, Statistics Canada reported men aged 65 have a better than 50% chance of living to 82.5 years of age and a 25% chance of reaching 89. Women aged 65 have a better than 50% chance of reaching 86 years of age and a 25% chance of living to 92. In addition, the odds are better than 50% that at least one member of a 65-year-old couple will live to see their 90th birthday and of those, one in four should live to reach 94.

Source: Statistics Canada, "Women and Men in Canada: A Statistical Glance – 2003 Edition

Age	80	85	90	95	100

Male age 65 — **83** ◀ 50% chance of living to 83 — **89** ◀ 25% chance of living to 89

Female age 65 — 50% chance of living to 86 ▶ **86** — **92** ◀ 25% chance of living to 92

Couple both age 65 — At least one person has a 50% chance of living to 90 ▶ **90** — **94** ◀ At least one person has a 25% chance of living to 94

The U.S. Census Bureau reports in 2030, nearly one in five US residents is expected to be 65 and older. This age group is projected to increase to 88.5 million by 2050, more than doubling the number in 2008 (38.7 million). Similarly, the 85 and older population is expected to more than triple, from 5.4 million to 19 million between 2008 and 2050.

Source: U.S. Census Bureau News, August 14, 2008 (CB08-123)

U.S. males who were 65 in 2005 are expected to live an additional 17.2 years and for women who were 65, they can look forward to an additional 20 years. Males who were 75 in 2005 are expected to live to 85.8 years and 75 year-old women, to 87.8 years.

Source: Health, United States 2007, U.S. Dept. of Health and Human Services, Publication No. 2007-1232

So what do all these numbers mean? Simply put, the population is getting older and people are living longer. Retirees have more time to plan, do and achieve the retirement they've been dreaming about. Where does one begin creating a successful retirement for life after work?

Right here. Right now.

An idea not coupled with action will never get any bigger than the brain cell it occupied.

~ Arnold Glascow ~

EXERCISE 1

I suggest you start by taking a few minutes to relax and visualize what the word "retirement" means to you. What is it about retirement that attracts, scares or excites you?

Now take a few minutes to write out your retirement life. What are you doing? What are your accomplishments? Be as descriptive as possible. Use additional paper if needed. To help you, consider the following questions.

In retirement:
- What makes me happy?
- How much money do I have?
- What possessions do I own?
- How am I spending my time?
- Who is in my retirement picture?
- How is my health? How do I feel?
- How are my relationships (spouse or partner, children, other family members)?

Try to visualize as much detail as possible. Don't be discouraged if your picture is fuzzy and lacking in detail at first. Clarity is close at hand.

In my retirement

_____

_____

_____

_____

_____

_____

_____

_____

Now imagine yourself specifically in your first six months of retirement. Then in one and two years. Does your mental picture change? If so, how? Take a moment and record your thoughts.

I'm imagining I've been retired for...

6 months

_____

_____

12 months

_____

_____

24 months

_____

_____

Now visualize yourself at the end of your retirement when you're 90, 95 or 100+. What are you most proud of? What have you done that brought happiness to you and others? What will you be remembered for?

Age

90 years old

_____

_____

95 years old

_____

_____

_____

_____

_____

Think about the people you know who have made a success of their retirement. What do they do that you admire? Is it their family relationships, their energy and enthusiasm, or perhaps their sense of being? Take a moment and record your observations.

_____

_____

_____

_____

Now think of those who are challenged by retirement. What are they doing or not doing that makes them, in your opinion, less successful in retirement? Is it the abnormal amount of time they spend watching television, their lack of adventure or possible sense of helplessness in an ever-changing world?

_____

_____

_____

_____

It has been said that the life we lead is a result of the choices we make. In your pre-retirement and retirement years, it's important for you to make the right choices – the ones that will result in building a fulfilling and energetic retirement. Visualization helps you create a mental model of retirement and helps to prepare you for making the right choices.

Frances, a busy 63-year-old supervisor, is employed with a major manufacturing company. Though for years she contributed to her Registered Retirement Saving Plan (RRSP), retirement wasn't part of her everyday *thinking. It was just something that would happen down the road.*

When Frances actually began thinking about retirement, she was at a loss as to what to do with the rest of her life. She didn't have a hobby, didn't like to exercise, she hadn't volunteered and had no interests outside of her work and family. For Frances, retirement appeared bleak and unappealing.

After receiving advice from a retired friend, Frances began to visualize what she wanted from retirement. She imagined herself as an above average tennis player (Frances played tennis in her 20s); she saw herself being fit and exercising regularly (Frances used to jog three times a week up until 10 years ago). She visualized herself performing some type of volunteer activity and giving back to her community. Frances began taking the first steps to building her retirement future.

Now that you have drafted a preliminary outline of your retirement, it's time to ask yourself if the plan will truly meet your needs and wants. We all know what we are retiring from - our job, boss, company, occupation or trade – but what are we retiring to? Is your retirement going to bring you the satisfaction you desire and deserve? To answer this question, you need to have a good idea of what will make your retirement life meaningful.

By being specific with your wants and needs, the choices you make along the way will be more goal-directed. You will recognize which behaviors and choices support your goals and which do not. You will also know when you are satisfying your needs and when you're off track.

The goal you set must be challenging. At the same time, it should be realistic and attainable, not impossible to reach. It should be challenging enough to make you stretch, but not so far that you break.

~ Rick Hansen ~

Most pre-retirees want, need and value family, their social life, financial security, health, personal and spiritual development and leisure. To find out what you want and need in retirement please complete Exercise 2.

EXERCISE 2 - PART ONE

Review each of the following common human needs and ask if it is important enough to be included in your retirement planning. If so, circle it and proceed to Part Two.

Achievement: Accomplishing tasks, being the best
Affection: Giving and receiving kindness, companionship
Affiliation: Being accepted, feeling a sense of belonging
Autonomy: Being my own person, establishing priorities and time schedules
Challenge: Getting involved in interesting and thought provoking endeavors
Competence: Being respected and recognized for skills and abilities
Expertise: Becoming a respected authority in something
Family: Having time and meaningful relationships with loved ones
Growth: Challenging oneself to be constantly learning and reaching full potential
Health: Being physically and mentally fit
Integrity: Being honest, true and conscious of oneself
Leadership: Able to willfully and responsibly direct and influence the efforts of others
Location: Enjoying current addresses, city, region, and country
Money: Being financially secure
Pleasure: Enjoying life, having fun
Recognition: Attaining status, being respected
Security: Leading a dependable and stable life
Service: Helping others, contributing to their well-being
Spirituality: Possessing inner harmony and peace, living by beliefs

Add other personal needs not listed.

_____

_____

_____

_____

_____

PART TWO

Now it's time to prioritize your list of needs. What need is most important to you? Which one ranks second? Prioritize your list below.

Need #1 _____

Need #2 _____

Need #3 _____

Need #4 _____

Need #5 _____

Need #6 _____

Need #7 _____

Need #8 _____

PART THREE

Visualize a retirement that meets your top six prioritized needs. Experience shows creating a vision with more than six needs is difficult and can lead to frustration and incompleteness. With your retirement vision, what are you doing, who are you with, what leisure activities are you participating in, what makes up your typical day, what is your diet like, what is your state of mind? Write your vision below.

_____

_____

_____

_____

_____

_____

_____

PART FOUR

Compare your retirement vision with your original retirement picture outlined in Exercise 1. Based on your prioritized needs, what changes are necessary, what additions or deletions are required to your original picture?

Additions or deletions to my original retirement picture:

_____

_____

_____

_____

Your vision of retirement should satisfy your personal wants and needs. If your retirement vision does not reflect what's important to you, then your retirement plans will be out-of-balance and the outcomes will simply not feel right.

A person who identifies 'health and fitness' as a highly important need must include appropriate measures to ensure that need is met in their retirement plan. Actions designed to achieve a healthy lifestyle may include a change in diet, regular exercise and the use of meditation techniques. Being healthy doesn't just happen - it takes work!

If you have a personal need for stability and security, then placing your retirement nest egg in risky financial ventures may result in sleepless nights and worry... neither of which you want as part of your retirement picture!

Investing in more stable financial instruments such as Guaranteed Investment Certificates (GICs), bonds and mutual funds, may give you a greater sense of security. Continuing to work in some capacity may also contribute to your need for stability.

Throughout the retirement visioning process, it is imperative to be optimistic about your future. Focus on the rewards of a balanced retirement. Enjoy feeling complete, being enriched and financially secure. Review and rewrite your retirement vision as often as required until it feels right and is in line with your wants, needs and beliefs.

When you have drafted your retirement vision, ask yourself the following questions:

1. Is my vision clear and understandable?   Yes   No
Remember, it's okay to have undefined parts of your retirement vision. These are just areas you have to think about further.

2. Is my vision brief or does it ramble?   Yes   No
Over time, your retirement vision will crystallize and be your guiding direction.

---

3. Does my vision have a primary focus?   Yes   No

Having a vision concentrating on meeting four to six important personal needs will be more manageable and achievable than if you were trying to meet eight or nine needs.

4. Is my vision flexible enough to change?   Yes   No

Recognize that your personal needs today may not be the same a few years from now. Down the road, you may require additional medical assistance and increased family support, which you may not need currently.

5. Does my vision serve as a guide that will help me make good decisions?   Yes   No

6. Does my vision reflect my values, beliefs and philosophy?
                                                       Yes   No

7. Is my vision representative of who I am?   Yes   No

8. Is my vision attainable?   Yes   No

If you build a retirement vision that is not realistic, you may set yourself up for failure.

9. Does my vision serve as a source for inspiration?   Yes   No

When you read and think about your vision, does it excite and give you positive feelings?

Recently, I spoke with a colleague named Bill and I asked him what his vision of retirement is. After a couple of minutes, he described his vision this way:

"I envision myself continuing in my profession but only working two days a week. My wife and I are having fun together, attending auctions, concerts and traveling. I am spending approximately one day a week doing volunteer work. I see myself curling twice a week in the winter and golfing once a week during the spring and summer. I am eating healthy meals and exercising

regularly. I envision my wife and I spending about 20% of our time with our children and grandchildren."

Bill has a clear and balanced vision of his retirement. His vision is brief and understandable. Bill's primary focus is Affection followed by Family, Health, Money, Pleasure and Service.

In the same week, I met a woman named Grace and when I asked her what her vision of retirement is, she answered:

"I don't know. All I know is that I'll be able to spend more time on my housework. Plus, I'll be able to watch the 'soaps' I've been missing when at work."

Perhaps this is Grace's ideal retirement. If this is truly her vision then it is easily attainable but may not be fulfilling. Without a carefully articulated vision, Grace will be doing housework and watching the 'soaps', six months from now and possibly six years from now. Without a more specific vision, Grace will get caught up in the endless trap of doing the same thing, in this case cleaning and watching television, over and over, until she dies.

The quality of your vision and your retirement is up to you. Once you have created your vision, share it with your spouse and several close friends. Explain to them in as much detail as possible what you're doing in retirement (i.e. continuing in your profession or trade), the new activities you are attempting, who you have as a support system, where you want to be living, your health and diet and all other aspects of who you are and where you want to be.

As you describe your vision, make note of what questions come to mind and those asked of you. Fill in the grey areas. Ask for suggestions on how you can achieve your retirement goals. Brainstorm ideas and solutions with those closest to you and record the findings. Take time to consider the input. Which suggestions make sense to you and which ones are unrealistic? Review your written vision and make changes as necessary. At the end of this process, you should have a clear picture of your retirement life. It is true that the visualization process and drafting of a balanced retirement plan take time and effort, but I can assure you, it is very worthwhile. A well thought-out retirement vision acts as your anchor and your compass for direction and future decisions.

EXERCISE 3

Based on the comments and suggestions of others, what additions or deletions will you make to your retirement vision?

_____

_____

_____

_____

_____

_____

_____

_____

_____

_____

This is the end of the chapter. Congratulations on taking the first step to a happy, successful and fulfilling retirement.

CHAPTER 2
CREATING A POSITIVE ATTITUDE

The greatest discovery of my generation is that man can alter his life simply by altering his attitude of mind.

~ William James ~

Now that you have crafted your retirement vision, the next step towards a successful retirement is to develop a positive attitude.

Fear, panic and discomfort are common emotions experienced by people preparing for retirement. These emotions often occur because the pre-retiree is entering a new world - one with different circumstances, behaviors and activities. It is a world filled with change, and with change comes opportunity! A successful retirement takes courage, commitment and desire. You can have an elaborate retirement plan but if you don't have the conviction to follow it, your plan is nothing more than words on a page. Change is a natural part of retirement. This involves changing routines, making new friends, trying new activities, and taking on new responsibilities.

For some people, retirement is so overwhelming they consciously or subconsciously sabotage their retirement plan by adopting a negative attitude. They accept the feeling that *'it's all over'*, that the changes required are too hard and they are likely to fail. They look back at their life remembering the *'good old days'* rather than welcoming the adventures that lie ahead. As a result of their negativism, they allow their health to deteriorate and lose their zest for life. They let negative emotions rule their actions and accept the retirement that just shows up. In doing so, they become the victim and use past events to make excuses.

Keith looked only at his past and refused to welcome the challenges of retirement. When he turned 65, he retired from his job and began receiving a pension. Soon after, Keith became bitter. He spoke only of his job and his work buddies whom he sees less and less. His negative attitude about 'growing old' and his complaints have driven away most of his friends. His children visit only when they have to and Keith spends many hours alone. Keith has turned his back on what may have been the best time of his life.

People with positive attitudes trust their abilities, are willing to take risks and believe in themselves. They look forward rather than backward, and they relish the future with a spirit of adventure. They choose the right behavior and the right thoughts to get the right consequences. They create the retirement they want!

So how do you create a positive attitude? The first step is to accept reality – your career is behind you. Don't dwell in the past; don't lament the things you didn't accomplish. Don't criticize yourself for the actions you didn't take.

Say to yourself out loud, *"The past is the past. It came and it went. So what can I do now to influence my present and future?"*

Creating a positive attitude means committing to yourself, getting involved in something worthwhile and continuing to grow in knowledge, skill and understanding. It is continually asking this question, *"What do I need to do to bring about the changes I want?"* It is viewing yourself as successful and having positive expectations for everything you do. The more positive images, questions, implicit beliefs and self-talk you engage in, the more positive your mind-set. If you catch yourself drifting into a negative mind-set, stop and refocus on the positive.

A positive attitude comes from surrounding yourself with positive people and having the will to keep trying until you get what you want. It's putting yourself at risk as you leave behind the comfortable and familiar to move onwards and upwards.

People with positive attitudes seek the humor in situations and can laugh at themselves. They believe with conviction that they deserve love and success. They open their heart and trust their ability to create a happy retirement.

Once again you have a choice. Be negative, repel others and look at the future with dread or be positive, attract like-minded people and view the future as a new and wonderful opportunity!

Choose now and say your choice out loud.

Pairing a well-formulated retirement vision with a positive attitude puts you well on your way to creating a rewarding retirement lifestyle. You are on the right track to actively molding your future.

Lisa accepts the challenges of retirement. When she left the workforce, her retirement vision was, and still is, to make good things happen. She welcomes each day and treats it as an adventure. As part of her journey she seeks out new people to meet and get to know, she plans one major trip a year, and spends time with her grandchildren. Lisa attends community concerts and often drives in the countryside with her camera looking for scenes to photograph.

Determined to have fun in her retirement, Lisa does it without spending a lot of money. Her zest for life is infectious and her positive attitude makes her delightful to be with. As a result, people gravitate to Lisa and her social circle keeps growing in quality and quantity. Lisa's assertiveness and confidence continues to build, as does her sense of purpose.

EXERCISE 4

Complete the Attitude Assessment on the following page. Read each pair of statements and rate yourself from 10 to 1. Circle the number representing where you currently are on the continuum. Upon completion, review your selected numbers. Note the areas with low scores (4, 3, 2, or 1). What changes do you want to make to increase your attitude in each of these areas?

Remember, this is your book. This is your plan. Be honest with your answers so you can get to your desired results quicker.

Attitude Assessment

	High Low	
Retirement is going to be the most exciting part of my life	10 9 8 7 6 5 4 3 2 1	I dread my retirement
There are many exciting opportunities after retirement	10 9 8 7 6 5 4 3 2 1	After retirement, everything is down hill
I want to stay in control and be active	10 9 8 7 6 5 4 3 2 1	I just want to withdraw from it
I will turn challenges into opportunities	10 9 8 7 6 5 4 3 2 1	I am not up to coping with change
I intend to expand my sense of humor	10 9 8 7 6 5 4 3 2 1	There's nothing fun about getting old
Retirees have advantages over others in society	10 9 8 7 6 5 4 3 2 1	Retirees have no advantages
I can make new friends	10 9 8 7 6 5 4 3 2 1	I'm obsolete, no one wants to know me
Retirement is the best time of life	10 9 8 7 6 5 4 3 2 1	This is the time to give up
Now I can use my creative talents and contribute	10 9 8 7 6 5 4 3 2 1	I have nothing to give

If you have been honest with your answers then continue to the next page.

Based on your responses to the previous statements, write out your action plan to increase your positive attitude towards retirement. Consider the following statements and feel free to include them in your plan.

• I will try to meet one new person each week
• I will laugh more and find the humor in situations
• I will view my retirement glass as half full, not half empty

_____

_____

_____

_____

_____

_____

_____

_____

_____

_____

_____

_____

_____

_____

_____

CHAPTER 3
HOW MUCH MONEY WILL YOU NEED?

How much money do you need to retire comfortably? Is it $250,000? $500,000? $1 million or more? What is a realistic amount based on your current and visualized lifestyle? Most people feel they need more money than what they have. Ask a person with $500,000 in retirement savings how much they need for retirement and nine times out of ten they will say, "More than what I currently have." Ask a person with $1 million or $3 million in retirement savings and the answer will be the same.

The monetary trick to a happy retirement is not to concentrate on amassing an abnormal amount of wealth, but to determine how much money will make you feel secure. In other words, how much money do you need to enable you to live and fulfill your visualized retirement lifestyle?

In a practical sense, how you spend your retirement time determines how much money you will need. If you plan to travel the world or indulge in expensive hobbies such as luxury sailing, then your financial needs will be much greater than someone with more modest plans. What you don't want is to envision a retirement you realistically cannot afford. All this does is cause anxiety and unease. By creating a retirement that is realistic and affordable, you gain satisfaction and peace of mind. Financially estimating your retirement plans is the key to determining the amount of money required.

PART 1

Ask yourself the following questions:

• At what age do my partner and I want to retire?

Me _____ My partner _____

- Are we planning to downsize our home? **Yes** **No**

- Will we move out of the city to a less expensive home in the country? **Yes** **No**

- Will we be moving to a retirement community? **Yes** **No**

- Do we want to rent or own a vacation home? **Yes** **No**

- Will we spend time in warmer climates each year and if so, for how long? _____ **Yes** **No**

_____

- Do we plan to travel abroad? **Yes** **No**
  How often and how far? _____

_____

- Will we be staying in upscale hotels? **Yes** **No**

- Do we plan any major purchases or renovations? **Yes** **No**

- Will I be working part-time while retired? **Yes** **No**

- Will I be helping to support any family members? **Yes** **No**

- What hobbies will my partner and I pursue and what are the costs?
  Hobby   **$**

_____   _____

_____   _____

_____   _____

_____

_____   _____

_____   _____

_____   _____

_____   _____

_____   _____

- Do we plan to frequently dine out,   **Yes**   **No**
  attend the theatre, movies?

- Do we plan to spend all our capital   **Spend it all**
  during our lifetime or are we planning   **Leave an estate**
  to leave an estate?

By answering the questions above, you should start to get a sense of how much money you will need in retirement. Obviously there is no single amount that will guarantee an adequate retirement.

Most financial advisors in North America use a guideline of 70 to 80% of current earnings to determine the amount you will need to maintain your standard of living in retirement. This is assuming that you are living mortgage or rent-free and that you will be able to live somewhat more inexpensively at this time.

Source: John Grobe, How Much Income Do You Need in Retirement, It Depends", FedSmith.com, Wednesday, July, 18, 2007

Notes:

_____

_____

_____

_____

_____

PART 2

As part of your financial plan, take a close look at what you may receive from Government Pensions and Old Age Security. Feel free to call the numbers provided to have your questions answered and obtain the information you need.

 A. Canada / Quebec Pension Plan (CPP/QPP)

The maximum CPP/QPP at age 65 in 2008 equaled $884.58 per month. You should determine how much you might receive from CPP/QPP from ages 60 through 65 and determine whether it makes economic sense to collect your CPP/QPP prior to age 65. Your financial advisor will be able to assist with your answer.

We recommend you submit your application for CPP/QPP as early as 12 months prior to the month in which you want your pension to begin. To qualify for the monthly CPP/QPP pension, you must meet one of the following criteria:

- You are 65 years of age or older
- You are between 60 and 65 years of age and have stopped working or have earnings from work below the maximum CPP/QPP retirement pension for two consecutive months

If you elect to receive your pension at age 60, your monthly payment will be 30% lower (6% a year for five years) than if you waited to age 65. However, by starting it sooner, you are likely to get the pension for a longer period of time. On the other hand, if you turn 65 and delay taking payments, the government will increase your benefit by ½% per month for each month you delay your claim; this is a permanent increase.

If you can wait to start your pension until age 70, your monthly payment will be 30% higher than if you took it at age 65. If you apply for it after age 70, retroactive benefits are only payable for a maximum of 12 months.

Government pensions are indexed for inflation. This means they rise each year to cover the cost of inflation and they are guaranteed for as long as you live.

To contact CPP in Canada or the United States, call:
1-800-277-9914 for service in English
1-800-277-9915 for service in French
or go to www.servicecanada.gc.ca for on-line services

To contact QPP in Canada or the United States, call:
1-800-463-5185
or go to www.rrq.gouv.qc.ca for on-line services

 B. Old Age Security

Old Age Security (OAS) is a basic benefit paid to all Canadians who are 65 and older and meet certain Canadian residency requirements. The maximum monthly amount paid in 2008 equaled $502.31. Depending on other income, you may have to give some or all of OAS back.

To apply for the Old Age Security pension, you can submit your application up to 12 months prior to your 65th birthday. If you are already 65 or older, send in your application as soon as possible so you won't lose any more payments.

For information on Old Age Security, call:
In Canada or the United States:
1-800-277-9914 for service in English
1-800-277-9915 for service in French
or go to www.servicecanada.gc.ca for on-line services

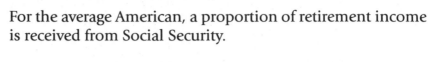

For the average American, a proportion of retirement income is received from Social Security.

To qualify for Social Security retirement benefits, you need a certain number of credits. If you were born in 1929 or later, you need 40 credits, which represents 10 years of work. Your benefit payment amount is based on how much you earned during your working career. Higher lifetime earnings result in higher benefits. In 2008, the maximum paid was $2,185 per month.

Your benefit payment also is affected by the age at which you decide to retire. If you retire at age 62, the earliest possible retirement age for Social Security, your benefit will be about 25% lower than if you wait until the 'full retirement age'.

For those born before 1938, the 'full retirement age' is 65. Due to longer life expectancies, the Social Security law was changed to gradually increase the full retirement age to 67. This change only applies to Americans born in 1938 and later.

Age to receive full Social Security benefits

Year of birth	Full retirement age
1937 or earlier	65
1938	65 and 2 months
1939	65 and 4 months
1940	65 and 6 months
1941	65 and 8 months
1942	65 and 10 months
1943-1954	66
1955	66 and 2 months
1956	66 and 4 months
1957	66 and 6 months
1958	66 and 8 months
1959	66 and 10 months
1960 and later	67

You may choose to keep working beyond your full retirement age. If you do, you can increase your future Social Security benefits.

Retirement benefits for widows and widowers

Widows and widowers in the United States can begin receiving Social Security benefits at age 60, or at age 50 if they are disabled.

Benefits for family members

If you are getting Social Security retirement benefits, some members of your family may also qualify for benefits. These benefits pertain to;

• Spouses who are age 62 or older
• Spouses who are younger than 62, if they are taking care of a child entitled on your record, who is under age 16 or disabled
• Former spouses, if they are age 62 or older
• Children up to age 18, or up to 19 if they are full-time students who have not yet graduated from high school
• Disabled children, even if they are age 18 or older

How do you sign up for Social Security?

You can apply for retirement benefits online at www.socialsecurity.gov or you can call toll-free 1-800-772-1213. You can also make an appointment to visit any Social Security office and apply in person.

Medicare

Medicare is a health insurance plan for people who are age 65 or older. Those who are disabled, have permanent kidney failure or have amyotrophic lateral sclerosis (Lou Gehrig's disease) can get Medicare at any age.

Medicare has four components:
1. Hospital insurance helps pay for inpatient hospital care and certain follow-up services

2. Medical insurance helps pay doctors' services, outpatient hospital care and other medical services
3. Medicare Advantage plans are available in many areas
4. Prescription drug coverage helps pay for medications prescribed by doctors for medical treatment

For more information, ask for Medicare (Publication No. 05-10043) or call Medicare toll-free at 1-800-633-4227.

 C. Guaranteed Income Supplement

The Guaranteed Income Supplement (GIS) payments are for eligible, low-income retirees. For the GIS you must be receiving the Old Age Security and meet specific income requirements. The maximum GIS paid monthly in 2008 was $634.02.

For information on Guaranteed Income Supplement payments, call:
1-800-277-9914 for service in English
1-800-277-9915 for service in French
or go to www.servicecanada.gc.ca for on-line services

For general information on Income Security Programs (disability benefits, survivor benefits, etc.) visit:
www.hrdc-drhc.gc.ca/isp for service in English
www.hrdc-drhc.gc.ca/psr for service in French

 Supplemental Security Income (SSI) is a Federal income supplement program funded by general tax revenues. It is designed to help aged, blind and disabled people, who have little or no income and it provides cash to meet basic needs for food, clothing and shelter.

For more information, contact Social Security
1-800-772-1213 • www.socialsecurity.gov

PART 3

Now it's time to review your company pension plan and benefits. Company plans are as varied as the companies that offer them. Become familiar with your company's plan, see what it offers and how it can add to the rest of your retirement income sources. At the same time, ask about the continuance of your company life insurance, medical, health and dental benefits when you retire. Lastly, if you have worked in another country, (i.e. United Kingdom), check with that country's pension authorities to determine your eligibility for a government pension.

PART 4

Determine what you have in savings, RRSP's, and Locked-in Retirement Accounts (LIRA's). List all income from non-registered investments as well. Be sure to look at: interest from personal savings, interest, dividends and/or redemptions from GIC's, mutual funds, stocks and bonds. Don't forget the conversion of home equity, income from business assets and real estate, and the liquidation of personal assets. Once listed, calculate your net worth using the upcoming Net Worth Statement form. Your net worth is the difference between what you own (assets) and what you owe (liabilities). It gives you a snapshot of your financial health at a specific point in time. Completing a net worth statement annually will help you assess your progress toward achieving your financial goals.

PART 5

Sit down and create a budget based on your retirement vision. Ask yourself if your budget is realistic and not exceeding, or limiting, your spending abilities. Review it regularly and make any necessary changes that will assist you in reaching your financial goals.

PART 6

Regularly review your budget, net worth, financial plan and overall financial goals. Take all necessary steps to consolidate any outstanding debt and initiate actions to reduce or eliminate your debt, including outstanding mortgages. We recommend that when your debts are paid off, you pay yourself a check for the amount previously going towards your debts. Deposit that check into a savings account every month. Also be sure to review your insurance plans with your agent or broker and adjust the coverage to meet your current needs.

PART 7

If you do not have a financial advisor, find one. Seek recommendations from friends, your banker, accountant, insurance agent and other people you trust and respect. Be sure to check the credentials and references of possible financial advisors. Confirm their educational background and professional affiliations. Ask yourself, *"Am I comfortable with this person and can I trust him/her with my money?"*

PART 8

Book and attend an appointment to review your government, company and pension benefits, as well as CPP/QPP, Old Age Security, Social Security/SSI, company pension and benefits, investments, budget, net worth and financial plans with your financial advisor.

PART 9

Explore whether converting part of your home equity into tax free money is a viable option. A reverse mortgage permits a homeowner 62 years of age or older, to qualify for 10% to 40% of your home's current appraised value. No payment is required as long as you and/or your spouse, continue to live in your home.

PART 10

Set aside 'fun money'. This is money you and your partner can use for special lunches, headline concerts, or a spur of the moment trip to see a good friend or family member.

When it comes to investments, no one has all the answers. You cannot predict beyond an educated guess, what the financial market will do. However, between you, your spouse or partner and your financial advisor, you increase the odds of making good financial decisions. Three heads are better than one!

Ron and Charlotte began making contributions to their RRSPs when in their early 40s. Until that time, their money was spent on mortgage payments, providing for themselves and their three children, paying off school debts and paying for other living expenses.

When they began seriously contributing to their retirement fund, they were afraid there would not be enough money for them to travel once a year to an exotic location, attend concerts, pay for Ron's golfing and Charlotte's photography hobby, help out their grandchildren with school and enjoy life in general. Ron and Charlotte believed the hype at the time stating that they would need over $1 million in savings to live comfortably.

After interviewing several financial advisors, Ron and Charlotte met Trevor. He was a financial advisor with whom they felt comfortable and he assisted Ron and Charlotte in constructing a reasonably sized RRSP portfolio. Over the years Trevor met with Ron and Charlotte to review their progress and assisted them with budgeting based on their envisioned retirement needs. When Ron retired at 65, he and Charlotte had over $700,000 set aside, which was enough to live comfortably and realize their retirement goals.

When asked about their progress, Ron and Charlotte admitted that without Trevor's professional advice and encouragement, they probably wouldn't have made the advances they did. If they handled their finances themselves, Ron and Charlotte figured they would have likely given up and convinced themselves they were destined to work their entire lives. Ron and Charlotte agreed even though they were relatively good money managers, they needed the outside advice and direction from Trevor to help them realize their long-term retirement vision.

Record the financial information discussed earlier:

Amount of government payments
you would receive
(i.e. CPP/QPP, OAS, Social Security)   _____

Employer pension plan benefits
you will receive at retirement   _____

Qualifying pension from
another country   _____

Notes:

_____

_____

_____

_____

_____

_____

_____

_____

_____

_____

_____

EXERCISE 5

Net Worth Statement

Step 1

	Current Value
A. Liquid assets	
Checking accounts	_____
Savings accounts	_____
GICs & T-Bills	_____
Cash value of insurance policies	_____
Money market mutual funds	_____
Other liquid assets	
(i.e. money owed to you, tax refunds)	_____
Subtotal	_____
B. Long term assets	
Mutual funds (non-money market)	_____
Stocks	_____
Bonds	_____
RRSPs/RRIFs/RESPs	_____
Company pension plan	_____
Subtotal	_____
C. Property assets	
Principal residence	_____
Vacation property	_____
Other real estate	_____
Vehicles	_____
Jewelry/art/collectibles/insurances/cash value	_____
Other property assets	_____
Subtotal	_____

Step 2

Liabilities

Mortgage (principal residence)   _____

Other mortgages   _____

Personal line of credit   _____

Auto loans   _____

RRSP loans   _____

Investment loans   _____

Credit cards   _____

Other loans   _____

Subtotal   _____

Step 3

Total Assets   _____

- Total Liabilities   _____

= Your Net Worth   _____

CHAPTER 4
MANAGING YOUR MONEY NOW

In addition to everything we've talked about so far, here a few things to consider from a money management standpoint, when creating your financial plan:

- Are you thinking of starting a business when you retire?
- Will you be moving?
- Do you want to travel extensively?
- Would you like to do something for your children or grandchildren?

Remember this is your vision and the amount of effort and level of detail you put into it now will pay off in the future. How much do you need to save? How much security do you want and are you able to budget effectively now so you can live happily on a reduced retirement income? Do the work today so you can enjoy retirement tomorrow.

A. Increasing Your Savings

Depending on your current financial position, you may be on target for the savings you need, or at least, somewhere close. For many people, paying off education loans, raising a family, making mortgage payments and life in general has not left them with much in the form of retirement savings. If you are 15 to 20 years away from retirement, you still have time to catch up. At your current stage of life with your children on their own and your house close to being paid for, you may have income available to make contributions to your savings. Here are six suggestions to make up for lost time:

1. Contribute the maximum to your RRSP
2. Take advantage of unused deduction room from previous years
3. Utilize the $2,000 over-contribution allowance to shelter additional funds from tax
4. When you have extra money resulting from a paid mortgage, put that money into your RRSP

5. Consider transferring non-registered investments into your RRSP
6. Consult with your financial planner before taking any action to ensure it is the right move for you

If retirement is close at hand, you can add to your retirement fund by the taking the following actions:

- Delay retirement until you are more financially secure. Working one more year may make a huge difference. Working part-time or starting a business may also assist with your retirement funding.
- You may have to save at a greater rate. Aggressive personal budgeting may be the answer.
- Consider downsizing your house or car, and re-evaluate your lifestyle expectations.

B. Annuities

Regardless of what stage of life you're in, most people like to have some security built into their retirement funding portfolio. One avenue to consider is investing in an annuity.

An annuity is a financial contract between you and an insurance company. You give them an amount of money in one lump sum and they agree to give it back to you in set amounts over a planned length of time. For example, with a 4-year annuity, a cash payment would be paid each year for four years at annual interest rates.

The attractiveness of annuities depends on interest rates. For example, if you purchased an annuity when rates were 10 to 12%, congratulations, you're doing well. Another advantage is having the guarantee of a reliable income from your assets without the hassle of managing a fund.

The different types of annuities are usually defined by their duration, such as:
- *Defined term annuities* – 5, 10 or 20 years. At the end of the term, the annuity is depleted and payments cease
- *Life annuities* – make guaranteed payments to you for the rest of your life

- *Joint-life annuities* – payments continue as long as you or your spouse is living
- *Fixed-rate annuities* – guarantee a stream of payments
- *Variable annuities* – offer flexibility with stocks, bonds and other investments
- *Prescribed annuities* – tax payments are spread over the life of the contract
- *Non-prescribed annuities* – tax payments decline each year of the contract

The type of annuity you choose should be based on your long-term goals, risk tolerance and your situation

Regardless of the type of annuity, payments are based on three key criteria:
1. The amount used to purchase the annuity
2. Interest rates at the time of purchase
3. Your life expectancy (and your spouse's if purchasing a joint-life annuity) at the time of purchase

You can receive payments monthly, quarterly, annually or any other interval agreed upon at the time of purchase. Once again, be sure to ask your financial advisor if purchasing an annuity makes sense for you.

C. The Importance of Budgeting

No matter where you're living or what you plan to do in retirement, you probably want at the very least, to maintain your present standard of living. To assist you in this process, personal budgeting is critical. Budgeting helps you determine where your money comes from, where it goes and how much is left over at the end of the month. It provides you with a clear picture of what your current lifestyle is costing you and your spouse, on a monthly basis.

If you're married, and only one person has been controlling the family expenses, it's time to change your system. Couples should work out cash plans together. Be sure to include all possible income and determine a realistic estimate of your combined expenses. The more you communicate and work together now, the less likely you are to have costly surprises later on!

EXERCISE 6

Complete the following Cash Flow statement forms. Evaluate the numbers and determine what changes are necessary to help achieve your retirement vision?

Cash Flow Statement

Cash Inflows	Monthly	Annually
Net salary (gross salary – taxes)	————	————
Interest income	————	————
Dividends	————	————
Capital gains	————	————
Rental income	————	————
Other income	————	————
(RRSP/RRIF or pension income,	————	————
Gov't. benefits, tax refunds)	————	————

Total inflows	————	————

Cash Outflows	Monthly	Annually
A. Living expenses		
Mortgage/rent	————	————
Property taxes	————	————
Heat	————	————
Water	————	————
Electricity	————	————
Cable TV	————	————
Telephone	————	————
Auto maintenance	————	————
Gas	————	————
Parking/transit	————	————
Groceries	————	————

Clothing   _____ _____

Childcare   _____ _____

Health and dental care _____ _____

B. Debt payments

Loan payments   _____ _____

Personal line of credit _____ _____

Credit cards   _____ _____

Other debt payments _____ _____

C. Insurance plans

Home   _____ _____

Auto   _____ _____

Medical/dental   _____ _____

Life   _____ _____

Disability   _____ _____

Other insurance plans _____ _____

D. Investment programs

Retirement contributions _____ _____

Education savings plan _____ _____

Emergency fund   _____ _____

Other investment programs _____ _____

E. Discretionary expenses

Entertainment   _____ _____

Vacation   _____ _____

Subscriptions   _____ _____

Membership fees   _____ _____

Gifts   _____ _____

Charitable donations   _____ _____

Household purchases   _____ _____

Tuition   _____ _____

	Monthly	Annually
Total cash inflows	_____	_____
Total cash outflows		
Total living expenses	_____	_____
Total debt payments	_____	_____
Total insurance plans	_____	_____
Total investment programs	_____	_____
Total discretionary expenses	_____	_____
Total cash outflows	_____	_____
Total cash inflows minus	_____	_____
Total cash outflows	_____	_____
Total savings available for goals	==========	==========

Notes:

_____

_____

_____

_____

_____

_____

_____

_____

CHAPTER 5
THE BEST TIME TO RETIRE

All of us were meant to be happy and successful. Life is more than a two-week vacation once a year. It is, and can be, exactly what you want it to be. There are no limits except those you put on yourself.
~ Thomas D. and Jane C. Willhite ~

As part of your retirement plan, you need to seriously consider the best time of year for you to retire. Not only are there financial implications to think about but you should also consider the season at the time of your retirement. Be sure to check the programs at your company before tendering your resignation.

A. Cost of Living

Some employer benefit programs state you must be retired on or before July 1st (meaning your last working day would be June 30) to receive any cost-of-living increase on your pension granted for July 1st. This means your on-going pension will actually be less if you retired in July or August compared with retiring on or before July 1.

B. Vacation Payoff

The first week of January may be appealing to begin your retirement, especially if you are carrying more than the maximum accrual for vacation. You could get paid for the total as long as you retire before the end of the first pay period in January. Retiring in January also gives you the entire tax year to absorb that lump-sum payoff.

C. Tax Considerations

Tax considerations and the best time to retire are different for each individual. It's worthwhile to estimate your taxes based on different dates throughout the year and I strongly recommend getting advice from a tax advisor a year or two before you plan to retire.

D. Season

Regardless of when you choose to retire, it is important to plan activities or events to counter or coincide with the season. For example, if you retire in January, you may want to start with a trip to the sunny south or take a ski holiday. However, if you choose to retire in the winter months (January – March), you may face many grey, cold, snowy days that can give the inaugural weeks of your retirement a bleak feeling.

Retiring in the spring (April – June) and the prospect of gardening and being outdoors may be appealing to you. Or perhaps you prefer the summer (July – September) and spending additional time at the cottage to officially launch your new life. The fall months (October – December) may be ideal as this is a time of completion, celebration and planning for the New Year.

When planning your retirement, decide the time of year that best suits you and your spouse from a financial, seasonal and goal perspective.

EXERCISE 7

Considering possible cost of living payments, vacation payoff, tax considerations and the seasons, choose the best time of year to begin your retirement and list the reasons for your choice.

_____

_____

_____

_____

_____

_____

_____

CHAPTER 6
HOW TO USE YOUR TIME

If you can imagine it, you can achieve it; if you can dream it, you can become it.

~ *William Arthur Ward* ~

Gone are the days of rushing to work, fighting traffic, meeting deadlines, hurried lunches and working overtime. Retirement is the time to slow down, blow off responsibilities, relax and play. This is your reward for all the years of hard work.

But how will you spend your time?

 In 2005, Statistics Canada reported Canadians aged 65 to 74 devoted on average, 7.8 hours a day for men and 7.2 hours for women, to leisure. About 4.1 of these hours for men and women were engaged in active leisure such as physical exercise, going out and socializing, while 3.7 hours for men and 3.1 hours for women were spent on passive leisure – watching television, listening to music or to the radio. Not surprisingly, Stats Can also found the least healthy and least satisfied retirees were those who spent the majority of their leisure time on passive leisure.

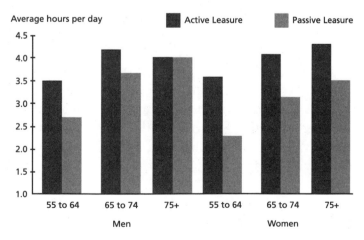

Time Spent on leisure by adults aged 55 and older, 2005

Source: Statistics Canada, Catalogue no. 89-622-XIE

At a time when the population of older adults in the US is growing rapidly, about a quarter of the adult population still reports achieving no leisure time physical activity. In a number of studies, it was found that self-efficacy and social support are important determinants of exercise and home-based physical activity. Overall, personal barriers included safety concerns, poor health, lack of time, motivation and energy as well as lack of skill. Environment barriers included lack of available places to engage in physical activity, no places to sit and rest during a walk, quality and availability of sidewalks and inclement weather.

Source: Role of Social Support & Self-Efficacy in Shaping the Leisure Tim Physical Activity of Older Adults, Journal of Leisure Research, Fourth Quarter, 2007,

Elizabeth M. Orseiga-Smith, Laura L. Pape

Improving one's self-efficacy can be accomplished by starting with small steps, observing others successfully perform the physical activity and obtaining verbal feedback and persuasion from family members, peers and leaders.

Source: Leisure expenditures of Retired and Near Retired Households, Journal of Leisure Research, First Quarter 2004, Robert O. Wesgley, Eunjeong Ho

The question for you now is - what are you going to do with your leisure time? Can you 'pull off' total leisure or will you need to blend it with some other activity such as volunteering or a part-time job? To help you with your decision, read the following descriptions for leisure, volunteering and working for money activities, and consider your wants, needs and preference.

A. Leisure

Are you the type of person who could spend retirement just doing leisure activities – playing golf, reading, playing bridge, going to movies or the theatre, or whatever else your heart desires? If so, then perhaps you feel you have all the money needed for retirement and you may be 'worked out' and never want to work again. It's also quite likely that you don't really want to volunteer or perhaps you're already 'volunteered out' from what you have given in your working days.

You may be a person who is not bothered by the thought of spending your days pampering yourself. Trust me, you've earned it! Perhaps your psychological makeup is such that you can relax for days at a time, without any self-pressure. You can see yourself traveling, watching or playing sports, shopping, taking naps and totally indulging yourself.

Martha is a single mother, who during her working life, held two jobs and studied at night for her certified accountancy designation. She volunteered at her church and helped with her children's school trips when time permitted. As Martha progressed in her working career, she vowed when she retired she would not work another day in her life, she would not be a volunteer, and retirement would be for her and her alone.

Is Martha being selfish? Maybe. Maybe not. It all depends on how you look at it. Imagine doing just one leisure activity, such as golfing or playing tennis, every day, month after month, year after year. At the beginning, it may sound like a dream to an enthusiast. However, after a few months of tennis as your only activity, you will probably find yourself bored, frustrated and developing a dislike for the game. You know the old saying - variety is the spice of life!

As a retiree you need to build a balanced leisure lifestyle so you don't fall into a rut. Though each person must design his or her own activity mix, consider a mix that includes at least one activity in each of the following leisure categories:

1. **Entertainment**
2. **Education**
3. **Travel**
4. **Sports**
5. **Social Activity**
6. **Hobbies**

1. Entertainment

Activities that fall under the 'entertainment' category include reading, attending concerts, watching your favorite television shows and dining out. Your plan may encompass each of these activities or you may pick one or two as part of your 'entertainment package'. For some people, reading one or more books a week is a great source of entertainment. For others, attending the symphony, opera, a movie or ballgame, is a marvelously entertaining event.

2. Education

In retirement, just as in life, you need to keep learning. This not only gives your brain stimulation, it provides you with a sense of adventure and discovery.

As part of your 'education' activities, you may consider:

a. learning a new language
b. learning a new craft
c. becoming expert in financial planning
d. becoming a history buff
e. studying genealogy

As you did with 'entertainment', consider adding at least one education activity to your leisure mix.

Miguel was born in Ecuador but grew up in Canada as a result of the immigration of his parents. Though Miguel's parents spoke both Spanish and English, they communicated primary in English to help Miguel with his assimilation into the Canadian school system. When Miguel retired he decided to learn Spanish, not only for his own interest but also as a way to better identify with his late parents and Ecuadorian heritage.

3. Travel

Another way to add variety to your leisure time is to travel. The opportunities available to retirees are numerous. Some people love to take a cruise a couple of times a year, while others participate in group tours to exotic destinations. For many, embarking on a long road trip or going camping satisfies the travel bug. How and where you travel is up to you. Many tour companies cater to the needs of the older traveler.

Discounts for seniors' groups range from airfares and hotel accommodations to car rentals and admission fees.

Careful planning is the key to trouble-free traveling. Help from a travel agent can be quite beneficial and for the most part, their services are free. Travel agents can provide up-to-the-minute information on fares and schedules, facilitate trip bookings and hotel reservations. In addition, they can assist with insurance coverage, passport and visa requirements, immunization needs, travel advisories and warnings.

For those who like to book their own trips and accommodations, there are many travel websites available to you and even a few are specific to seniors including: www.seniortravel.about.com, www.eldertours.com and www.seniorsgotravel.com.

4. Sports

Every retiree should have at least one sport component to his or her leisure plan. Whether you like to hike, bike, golf, swim, fish, play tennis, or power walk, we can all benefit from some activity that helps us stay physically fit. Remember when choosing your sport, think about one for the spring and summer months as well as one for winter. You may choose lawn bowling, hiking or fishing for the warm season and snowshoeing, skiing or ice fishing for the colder months. One complaint often heard is, "I love the warm months because I am outside and active but in the winter, the time drags because I'm indoors most of the time." Obviously, living in Canada and the northern United States, we all need some kind of activity that gets us outside in the winter to help us enjoy our cold but beautiful, snowy climate.

When Eva retired, she gave considerable thought to taking up a sport. Traditionally she wasn't an active person so she talked to friends regarding their sporting choices and why they enjoyed them. After considering the possibilities, Eva decided to participate in women's bowling and group power walking. As a result, she has more energy and drive plus she enjoys the camaraderie and friendship of her fellow sports enthusiasts.

5. Social Activities

Interacting with others is important at all stages of life, and especially as we age. As part of human nature we are social beings and it's the activities involving others that help us meet our social needs. Most people don't realize the extent to which co-workers help fill the basic need for socialization – the water cooler chats, lunchtime gab fests, coffee breaks or grabbing a drink after work. We've built friendships, shared common interests and enjoyed each other's company.

When we retire from a job, we leave many of these associations behind. It is important to replace, as best as possible, the shared times with other social activities that provide us with the fellowship we enjoyed while at work.

You may consider joining a service club such as the Lions or Rotary, a special-interest group, a social club or simply arranging a regular game of cards with family or friends. You could go dancing, visit with relatives, or attend bingo, anything that gets you out of the house into a social setting. The important thing is to get out there and participate, socialize, meet new people and make new friends.

Clare felt lost when she retired from her job as a librarian of 27 years. Not only did she enjoy helping people meet their information and reading needs, she loved the discussions with fellow librarians over a coffee or lunch. She missed the political debates, talking about community events and projects, and of course, the banter over individual interests, hopes, dreams, hobbies and families.

After settling into her retirement, Clare realized the importance of other's company. As a way to fill her need for companionship, she joined a reading club. Each week club members meet for breakfast and discuss the books they have read. Not only was Clare totally at home talking about books, she expanded her literary knowledge and developed several close friendships.

6. Hobbies

I encourage you to go to any hobby store and walk the aisles. The selection of potential hobbies knows no bounds. As part of your leisure planning, consider finding at least one hobby that interests you. Be enthusiastic and choose an activity that gives you pleasure and is engaging without being overly time consuming.

One of the greatest benefits of a hobby is experiencing the pleasure of working at something interesting, without having an obligation to do it. There are no time schedules or demands for completion; it is just something to do for fun. Ask a photographer why he/she enjoys their photographic hobby and you will hear words such as *"It helps me see the world in a different way"*, *"Hearing the click of my camera shutter is such a wonderful sound"*, *"When I'm taking pictures, time just disappears"*.

Some hobbies lend themselves to providing income and may even develop into second careers. The secret to finding the right hobby is your ability to thoroughly enjoy the activity. Look for something that gives you a sense of purpose and accomplishment.

The following is an example of some hobbies you could consider:

Genealogy	Stamp or coin collecting
Oil painting	Furniture refinishing
Folk art	Sculpture
Antique collecting	Needlepoint
Trout fly tying	Flower arranging
Gourmet cooking	Wine tasting
Gardening	Car restoring
Model building	Woodworking
Photography	Paper tole

Finding the right combination of entertainment, education, travel, sports, social activities and hobbies to match your life style and personality takes time and effort. Be prepared to experiment with your leisure activity selection until you find the right mix. The trap of not creating a balanced leisure life is procrastination. Though most of us realize the importance of having various interests, we sometimes tell ourselves, "I'll start my search next month" and next month never comes. Don't put off your search! Start checking out the fun stuff and get building your leisure plan today!

John, a train engineer, and his wife Rita, an accountant, recently retired. Both believe they have a balanced leisure life. John loves to build model railroads and is an avid reader of novels and biographies. Rita has a passion for gourmet cooking and enjoys her stock market group. Together they attend a concert once every three months and watch several of their favorite television shows. They dine at a local restaurant once every two weeks and enjoy long walks through the neighborhood. They travel every year and have recently planned a trip to Morocco. John golf's in the warmer months and joined a senior men's curling league that has him on the ice twice a week in the winter. Rita keeps in shape by working out at a local gym. Both John and Rita spend time with their families including their six grandchildren. John has developed an interest in woodworking and is saving up to buy a router. As a couple and individuals, John and Rita are happy with their 'leisure plan' as it brings them satisfaction and variety.

EXERCISE 8

Considering your retirement leisure lifestyle, list your current activities in each of the six leisure areas. What activities do you plan to explore?

My Leisure Activities

	Current Activities	**Activities I will explore**
Entertainment	_____	_____
	_____	_____
	_____	_____
Education	_____	_____
	_____	_____
	_____	_____

Travel _____ _____

_____ _____

_____ _____

Sports _____ _____

_____ _____

_____ _____

Social Activities _____ _____

_____ _____

_____ _____

Hobbies _____ _____

_____ _____

_____ _____

> *It is not what we get. But who we become, what we contribute*
> *... that gives meaning to our lives.*
>
> *~ Tony Robbins ~*

B. Volunteering

Many retirees tell you the one thing they miss most from their working lives is the structure. It's the need to get up in the morning, be at work for a certain time, attending meetings, solving problems, to be with people and have a sense of accomplishment. If you crave structure then volunteering may be for you. By being a volunteer you are able to give back through your time and talents, to the benefit of others. It may be a fulfilling way to be involved and get the structure you are looking for.

As human beings we have a strong need to help others. It makes us feel important and that we are contributing to something larger than ourselves. Volunteering gives the feeling of being needed, useful and it provides us with a sense of purpose. We gain gratification in seeing others develop and succeed. We get a tremendous sense of pride while at the same time earning the respect of others.

Volunteering can also be protection from post-retirement let down. Often times, a newly retired person has a list of tasks they plan to do. "When I retire, I'm going to remodel my house"; "I'm going to catch up on my reading"; "I'm going to work on my car". Six months later, when they've completed the to-do list, a post-retirement disappointment settles in. Volunteering gives you a fighting chance against retirement let down.

Volunteering can help keep your mind active and enhance your leisure hours. It offers you a chance to contribute in an experience where you aren't tied to the role as you may be or have been in a 'money-job'. With a volunteer assignment, you can come and go more easily. If, for instance, you and your partner want to spend your summers at the cottage, it's relatively easy to put your volunteer activities on hold for two or three months.

Through volunteering you also meet compatible people, people with similar interests and perspectives to your own. This can lead to the development of new friendships. It also enables you to showcase your professional or trade skills and provide opportunity to learn new ones.

Recognition from volunteering often comes from those you are helping and the organization you are working with. Non-profit organizations recognize the value of their volunteers and go to great lengths to express their appreciation. This can range from a simple "thank you" to holding events, publishing special notes of recognition in organization newsletters, awarding service pins and plaques and the like.

Mary was a hospital administrator prior to her retirement. Currently she is working as a volunteer with several community health clinics helping them to update their clinic procedures and policies. In the process, Mary is learning about the health challenges facing clinic staff working in multi-cultural communities and the importance of outreach programs.

Many retirees report that volunteering helped them find a second career.

Alicia loves gardening and volunteers with her local botanical center. Over the years, Alicia has learned a great deal about garden design and horticulture. When she retired, a number of friends and acquaintances asked for her advice on gardening and garden design. As a result, Alicia now operates her own thriving garden boutique specializing in small garden design.

The options for volunteering are limitless. Examples of volunteer activities are:

- Teaching English as a second language
- Assisting new immigrant children with math and other school subjects
- Assisting in local art galleries, museums and zoos
- Volunteering in local hospitals
- Working with disadvantaged youth
- Delivering meals to shut-ins
- Counseling young mothers
- Participating in housing programs like Habitat for Humanity

When considering volunteering as an option, ask yourself, "How much time do I want to commit?" Is it three hours a day, one morning a week, or two days a week? Once you decide what makes sense for you and your spouse, stick to your time allocation until you're both sure you can handle more.

You also need to learn to say no. Unfortunately, volunteer organizations are constantly looking for additional help. It is easy to find yourself bombarded with volunteering requests that you commit to and then become overwhelmed. If the request for your time and talents is just too much, feel free to say, "Thanks, but no thanks".

No matter what your career skills or background experience, find your own volunteering niche. You may want to first try different volunteering experiences to help determine what type of volunteer work best suits you. If you are interested in volunteering, contact your local library or the Internet under 'Volunteering' for contact names and organizations specializing in placing new volunteers. Here are some suggested websites to visit when considering your volunteering options.

http://new.volunteer.ca   www.givingandvolunteering.ca

www.unitedway.ca   www.altruvest.org

www.volunteermatch.org   www.pointsoflight.org

www.ceso-saco.com

EXERCISE 9

List the organizations or activities you would be interested in volunteering with. Select one or two you plan to contact regarding volunteer opportunities.

Organizations/activities that interest me	Action plan
i.e. My place of worship	In the next week I will contact my religious leader about volunteering

C. Working at a Money Job

For some, the thought of working in retirement is foreign and outright rejected. For others, especially those who may not have sufficient savings or who love to work, being gainfully employed after retirement is quite attractive. For these people, paid work represents an acknowledgement of their self-worth and contribution, while for others it is an opportunity to have new colleagues and workmates.

Many retirees work reduced hours in their respective profession or trade. Employers are becoming more amenable to continuing employment of their senior employees, either on contract or limited working hours. If you are interested in continuing to work for your employer after retirement, speak to your Human Resources representative about the possibilities.

Though you may not wish to continue working on a regular basis for your employer, you may be open to part-time or seasonal work, of which there are many opportunities. You could work retail during Christmas or at a lakeside resort in the summertime. Perhaps you want to work with children and have summers off, build fences, become a baby sitter, gardener, postal worker, substitute teacher, researcher or writer.

One of the benefits of a paid job is the appreciation of leisure hours. With a paying job, there is a greater need to plan and manage your leisure time. Retirees report money-jobs help eliminate their down periods especially if they have too much leisure time on their hands. Another reported benefit is the therapeutic value of keeping mentally and physically sharp.

In today's employment environment, there is a great demand for older workers. Companies are very willing to hire older people as it often means spending less time, energy and money on orientation and training of the new employee. Many employers view retirees as steady and more reliable than younger workers and older workers require less time off. Retirees traditionally have a strong work ethic and are often able to work flexible hours during the day. This makes them a good source of people power for relief work on weekends, vacations and sick-time.

To get yourself ready to land a job, first you need to update your resume. Then check the help-wanted ads and on-line job placement websites such as www.workopolis.com and www.monster.ca. Contact a commercial employment agency and tell your friends and associates you are willing and available to work. Stay informed by reading the business pages of your newspaper and the trade publications for who's hiring. For the companies you like, check out their websites for vacancies. Regularly assess your skills as to what you can offer an employer and always project a positive attitude and willingness to learn.

Some Canadian provinces have legislation preventing age discrimination of those over 65. The legislation protects your right to be offered the same opportunities in employment, promotion and training as everyone else. In addition, your age should not be used against you in hiring or promotion opportunities. On the flip side, your age should not be used to force you into retirement. Check with your provincial/state Human Rights Commission as to age discrimination legislation in your area.

April was a nurse in a busy city hospital. When she retired, she took time off to simply unwind and relax. After a couple of months, April felt the urge to return to nursing and she approached her previous employer about working part-time. Her employer jumped at the chance and now April works two night shifts per week. Her part-time nursing job provides April with additional income plus her working schedule permits time to enjoy both her leisure and volunteer activities.

As a second option, you may be interested in starting your own business in any one discipline such as: consulting, home decorating, small engine repair, tax form completion, senior care, child care, furniture restoration, dog walking, tutoring, cake decorating, caretaking, organizational coach, garage sale convener, hairstylist, pet sitter, bicycle repair, or even wedding or event planner. If you're interested in starting your own business, then visit www.canada-grants-loans.org or www.sba.gov in the US. These websites contain information on available business grants and loans.

One of the first steps when considering the start up of your own enterprise is to develop a business plan. Your plan will act as a good management tool and an important key to raising needed capital to get your business off the ground. Ensure your business plan showcases your product or service. It should show how you plan to make a profit and when. It should also include market data and trends to show the need for your product or service. Be sure to list projected costs and sales, a break-even analysis and long term goals. For samples of business plans, visit www.bplans.com.

EXERCISE 10

Answer the following questions based on your personal needs. If you have six or more 'yes' answers, you should consider either a paying job or starting a business as part of your retirement plan.

	Yes	No
1. I have a strong work ethic that needs to be satisfied	____	____
2. I need to feel I've accomplished something each day; only a money job will fulfill my need	____	____
3. Working for money is important to me	____	____
4. I need a money job to wake up to	____	____
5. Work keeps me in the mainstream and in contact with others in my profession or trade	____	____
6. Work keeps my mind active	____	____

7. I need the money ___ ___

8. Working part-time will help me enjoy my leisure
time more ___ ___

9. Work is pleasure for me – as long as I get paid for it ___ ___

10. Work is therapeutic; it will keep me alive longer ___ ___

Total Score: ___ ___

Based on what you've read in this chapter list three or four work options that interest you:

_____

_____

_____

_____

CHAPTER 7
HEALTH AND WELLBEING

One of the greatest discoveries a man makes, one of his great surprises, is to find he can do what he was afraid he couldn't do.

~ Henry Ford ~

Many people contemplating retirement believe it is a time to throw your cares away, just relax and smell the roses. True, retirement is a time when you focus more on yourself and it's a time when work priorities change. However, keeping healthy should be part of every person's journey into retirement.

Being healthy means having good physical, mental and spiritual well-being. The interesting thing is when you are well you have a feeling of vitality and personal confidence. And when you are unwell, you feel tired, lethargic and down in spirit. Building a strong sense of wellness means spending time assessing your current state of health and asking, "What can I do to improve my wellbeing?" Obviously you need to get regular physical checkups and work with your doctor in developing a wellness plan that makes sense for your age and body. You need to create and follow a regular physical exercise routine. You also need to eat the right foods in the right proportions, and develop a healthy frame of mind.

GREAT GRUNTS...NEXT WEEK WE'LL TRY WITH SOME WEIGHTS!

Realistically, you cannot stop the aging process but you can slow it down. By taking control of your wellness, you can reduce the risk of some serious diseases such as cancer and heart disease. You can increase the odds of living longer, reduce the amount of money you pay out in medical costs and improve the quality of your life. You can influence the course of your own health and life by educating yourself, staying active, and following practical and sensible health and nutrition guidelines.

Consulting with your doctor should be part of your retirement planning. Ask for a complete physical exam including appropriate laboratory testing. Talk to him or her about your current physical and mental health and get information on appropriate physical exercises you should be doing given your health and age. Discuss your diet and enquire about preventive immunizations including annual flu shots. Due to possible time constraints, your doctor may not be able to answer all your questions in one visit so make arrangements to continue the discussion at a second visit.

An essential part of your overall wellness plan is having regular eye and hearing tests, mammograms, prostate exams and pap smears. You also need to visit your dentist every six to nine months and practice good oral hygiene. Remember without your health, all the retirement time and money is not much good if you are unable to spend it accordingly to plan.

A. Physical Wellness

Regular exercise is a major contributor to your overall wellness. Physical activity is a part of what makes us alive and keeping active grows more and more important as you age. Exercise improves cardiovascular efficiencies, lowers blood pressure, strengthens bones, builds muscle strength and improves metabolism. Without activity, you will deteriorate at a rapid rate, which increases exponentially as you get older. Other benefits of regular exercise are weight control, balance and flexibility.

A good physical exercise program helps you feel better about yourself and protects your body from disease, fatigue and lethargy. A complete exercise program will help you transmit a better image to others and give you more confidence.

The key to developing a program that is right for you is to choose the right activities. If you do not enjoy what you are doing, your commitment to exercise will dwindle. Luckily there are hundreds of options for activities that will elevate your heart rate, help with weight control and build muscle. For some people, brisk walking is a good choice, while others may prefer swimming. If you like to be outdoors in all types of weather, then power walking or running may be good exercises for you. However, if you dislike being out in the cold, perhaps an indoor calisthenics program would be better. If you are concerned with your body shape and weight and are self-conscious about wearing a bathing suit, then obviously swimming may not be a good choice and tennis, golf or lawn bowling may better suit your personal comfort needs.

When choosing an activity to include in your plan, ask yourself:

• Are there any physical activities I am afraid of?
• Would traveling long distances to participate be a deterrent?
• Am I a health club type of person?
• Do I like, or dislike competitive sports?
• Am I a person who needs encouragement of others to get me involved?
• Am I more comfortable exercising on my own?
• Do I enjoy physical activities that require time to master new techniques? (i.e. Yoga, Tai-Chi, Pilates)

Be sure to try a variety of different activities before committing to one. During your testing period, refrain from buying expensive equipment in case the activity you thought is 'great!' turns out to not be. Try to rent or borrow the needed equipment until you are totally convinced it is the right activity for you.

Heidi joined a tennis club on the advice of a friend as a way to be active and spend more time together. Upon signing up, she also purchased 12 lessons from the club pro. She bought herself an expensive tennis racket, several tennis outfits, top-of-the-line tennis shoes and a few other accessories. Heidi attended her first couple of tennis lessons and tried to enjoy the experience of learning a new game but by the fourth lesson, Heidi knew that tennis wasn't for her. Heidi's tennis equipment now sits gathering dust in her closet and her remaining paid lessons unused.

Here is a short list of the more popular physical activities for you to consider:

- Walking
- Swimming
- Bicycling
- Low-impact aerobic classes
- Tennis
- Lawn bowling
- Racquetball
- Cross-country skiing
- Curling

After choosing one or more physical activities, create a schedule that enables you to fit it/them in. If need be, get a friend or neighbor to join you so you can encourage and support each other. Share your training targets and desired weight goals with your doctor to ensure they are realistic.

The secret to having a fit body is consistency. Normally, you should exercise a minimum of three days a week and 30 minutes each time. Be sure to set goals and track your progress. Ask yourself, *"In three months, what would I like to be accomplishing? Is this realistic given my current state of fitness?"* Remember to establish 'stretch' goals: ones you need to work at to achieve but don't set yourself up for failure by raising the bar too high. Keep them realistic for your age, body type and strength and endurance level.

Keeping a record of your results accomplishes two things. One, it shows progress towards your goals and two, it acts as a motivational tool to keep you going.

Since we lose strength and elasticity as we age, build in five or ten minutes of calisthenics as part of your exercise program. Exercises such as arm rotations, sit-ups, toe touches, stretching from side to side, and leg thrusts are very beneficial. I know I told you not to rush into buying new equipment but I am making an exception in this case. Go and purchase a pair of five- and ten-pound weights, then regularly use them as part of your exercise program. Weight training will help you maintain and increase your body strength.

Share your exercise regimen with family and friends and ask for their encouragement. When you meet your goals, tell people what you have accomplished and let them know what you're planning for the future. This builds momentum and earns accolades, both of which act as a stimulus for achieving future physical fitness success.

Once you get into a pattern of exercising and begin feeling the results, stay in tune. Give this part of your day top priority. When traveling, develop substitute exercises and when illness strikes, tell yourself you will immediately return to your exercise regime when you are well enough to do so.

When Bill was 63, he contemplated retiring on his 64th birthday. He consulted with his financial planner and accountant and each told him he had sufficient savings in his RRSP and other money accounts to be able to live a comfortable, though not lavish, retirement lifestyle. Bill then turned his thoughts to his physical health. Though he considered himself in reasonable shape, he noticed he was getting tired faster and was taking more time than usual to recuperate from business trips or illnesses.

Bill then looked in the mirror and admitted to himself, he was not in the best physical condition. Right there, Bill made a commitment - if he was going to enjoy his retirement to its fullest, he would have to devote time and energy on becoming physically well.

After consulting with his physician, Bill began walking regularly. He set a goal of walking briskly for 20 minutes twice a week. At first, he thought he had set his goal too high but he persisted despite his doubts. Within two weeks, Bill was walking 30 minutes, three times a week. After four weeks, Bill was walking four times a week for 40 minutes each time. Bill was beginning to feel more energetic. He felt calmer and his over-all confidence increasing. Bill then bought five and 10 pound dumbbells and began an easy weight-training program aimed at giving him better muscle tone. After three months of walking and weight training, Bill was getting compliments on his appearance and energy level. People who had not seen him for some time observed he looked and sounded healthier and younger than the old Bill.

Bill has now begun his retirement and he says he has not felt better in his life. He keeps up his physical fitness and is training for a ten-kilometer run.

EXERCISE 11

List the physical activities you currently do or would like to try. Write down why they appeal to you. For activities you would like to try, set a time frame for when you are going to start each activity. For activities you already engage in, set new goals for accomplishment.

Physical Activities I do or would like to try	Why I like or think I would like this activity	My goal(s) is:
Brisk walking, 30 min. four times a week	I'm not tied to a specific time or place	In two months I will walk five times a week, 40 min. each time

B. Diet and Nutrition

As you get older, your nutritional needs change. Your metabolic rate, the speed at which your body burns calories, tends to decline. This means your body needs fewer calories to perform basic bodily functions such as walking, breathing and talking. This also means you need to eat less or you may put on weight.

As you age, you have to become more nutrition conscious, which means knowing what are the right foods for your body. The typical North American diet is full of refined carbohydrates combined with highly processed meats. Lunchtime for many people means a hamburger or cold cuts. The only vegetable to be found in such a meal is some lettuce and/or ketchup.

The most common challenge for mature people is the need to reduce the amount of fat consumed. This requires reading food labels for both fat and calorie content. It also means, as your parents taught you, eating plenty of fruits, vegetables and whole grain foods. In addition, limiting the amount of red meat you consume and increasing the baking, broiling, steaming or sautéing of your foods rather than frying. Due to the high cholesterol content in eggs and dairy products, eggs need to be used in moderation or replaced with an egg substitute; and make the switch from whole to skim milk.

When developing a healthy diet, reduce your sugar, butter and salt intake as each of these can increase your risk of weight gain, clogged arteries or higher blood pressure. Remember to drink plenty of water – six to eight glasses per day - and limit your intake of coffee, tea and soft drinks as they dehydrate your body.

Most, if not all essential nutrients are altered to some degree, by food processing. Be sure your diet includes vitamins or nutritional supplements. Before trying to decide what your body needs in the form of vitamins and supplements, consult with your doctor regarding the products he/she recommends given your health history and body type.

Here are a few tips from Canada's Food Guide for good eating:

- Eat at least one dark green and one orange vegetable a day
- Have vegetables and fruit more often than juice
- Make at least half of your grain products whole grain each day
- Drink skim, 1% or 2% milk each day. Eat yogurt or drink fortified soy beverages if you do not drink milk
- Have meat alternatives such as beans, lentils or tofu often
- Eat at least two servings of fish each week
- Enjoy foods with little or no added fat, sugar or salt
- Limit foods and beverages high in calories, fat, sugar or salt
- Satisfy your thirst with water

When shopping for groceries, add cabbage, brussel sprouts, turnips, broccoli, peas, carrots, sweet potatoes, spinach, nuts and seeds, mushrooms, berries, bran cereals and olive oil to your shopping cart. Read up on foods and nutrition so you will be educated as to what is best for your diet. Try not to indulge too often on highly processed foods and/or cookies, cakes, white bread or buns. Lastly, try not to shop at mealtime or when you're hungry.

Cook fresh food. Steam your vegetables and remove skin from chicken and fat from beef. Grill, roast or poach meat and fish. Add herbs or spices instead of salt. If you have food allergies, you can substitute barley, brown rice or spelt for wheat and almond or walnut butter for peanut butter. Vegetarians can substitute lentils, beans, tofu, eggs and dairy for meat and fish. Serving sizes are important. Eyeball your servings; 1 teaspoon of butter equals a fingertip, ½ cup of cooked vegetables is about the size of your fist and a thin fish fillet is the size of a checkbook.

The following is a sample of a healthy menu:

Breakfast: ½ cup oatmeal, ½ cup milk, ½ cup berries
Snack: apple and yogurt
Lunch: spinach salad, whole grain pita, 2 oz. lean meat or fish, fruit
Snack: handful of walnuts or 1 oz cheese with whole grain crackers

Dinner: 1-cup carrots and broccoli stir-fried in olive or canola oil, 3 oz
            lean beef or chicken, steamed brown rice

As part of your personal development, visit your public library and browse some books about diet and nutrition. Visit Canada's Food Guide website for food serving recommendations and meal planning www.hc-sc.gc.ca. Remember, you are what you eat!

Mary Lou taught mathematics and history at a local high school. She also taught photography at a nearby community college. She was 2 years away from retirement when she first thought about her diet and nutrition. Mary Lou admitted that she had been abusing her body. Due to a very hectic work schedule, her lunches and dinners consisted of tacos, burgers and other assorted junk food.

In preparation for retirement, Mary Lou stopped eating junk food 'cold turkey'. She now eats a balanced diet consisting of plenty of fruits and vegetables. She reduced her intake of red meats and starchy foods. She also drinks, on average, six glasses of water a day and limits her caffeine intake to one coffee in the morning and one tea in the afternoon. Recently she began drinking green tea for its antioxidant properties and takes a liquid nutrition supplement. Due to her dietary changes, Mary Lou has lost 10 pounds, feels more energetic and has a clarity of mind she has not felt in years.

EXERCISE 12

Considering your current diet, what changes will you make to help you lead a more robust and enjoyable life? What foods are you going to eat more of and which ones are you going to cut back on?

Changes I am going to make in my diet:

_____

_____

_____

_____

_____

_____

_____

I am going to eat:

More of:	**Less of:**
bran cereals	donuts and muffins
lean meats	processed meats
raw vegetables	over-boiled vegetables

_____ _____

_____ _____

_____ _____

_____ _____

_____ _____

_____ _____

My weight target in one month, three months, six months is:

My weight target in one month: _____

My weight target in three months: _____

My weight target in six months: _____

_____

C. Mental Health

In our society, work is a defining feature of our daily lives and to a large extent, our identity. It is more than the mental and physical tasks we perform. Work refers to the idea of being paid and engaged in activities that are productive. Making up such a substantial part of your being, ending your work life may not be an easy task. When you are working, your day is outer-directed. You focus on the task at hand and are normally busy for eight hours a day. Time is measured in what you have accomplished, whether it is the report you completed, the clients visited, the number of parts produced or meetings attended. When you retire, your day becomes inner-directed. You alone must plan your day and week. Success depends on your ability to find happiness in satisfying personal interests and pursuits, human relationships and creative mental activities.

As you approach retirement, you may have fears about possible loss of self-identity or esteem, financial worries and concerns about your health. For many newly minted retirees, the first months can be difficult because of our strong identification with 'work'. Just sitting back and reading the newspaper can result in a sense of guilt or anxiety because it doesn't feel like you are doing anything valuable and productive.

Upon entering retirement, you may experience butterflies, sweaty palms, upset stomach and free-floating anxiety. First of all relax. These are normal reactions to the new roles you are adopting. However, when stress builds up, your body reacts.

Here are some possible symptoms of distress or stress overload:

• Tension headaches
• Numerous colds, cold sores and other viral disorders
• Skin rashes
• Ulcers and digestive disorders
• Irritability
• Insomnia
• Heart palpitations, high blood pressure

- Depression and grief
- Accidental injury due to inattention or distraction

As a cautionary note, if you suffer one or more of these symptoms, consult your doctor.

Stress. You've had it before and chances are you will have it again. So what do you do when you experience stress? Just knowing that retirement brings change that may cause you stress, is a crucial first step in coping. When you experience increased stress, you can take action to reduce it and keep it in check. Relaxation is one of the most powerful weapons you have to fight increased levels of stress.

Relaxation Techniques:

A. Physical exercise. For many people, just the simple act of exercising (i.e. walking, jogging, or playing tennis) is sufficient to reduce or eliminate their stress.

B. Deep breathing. One way to help reduce stress, lower your heart rate and blood pressure is to breathe deeply. Take a deep breath through your nose, hold it for ten seconds and release it slowly through your mouth. Repeat the process for five minutes.

C. Progressive muscle relaxation. Find a comfortable place where you can stretch out and relax. This may be on a couch, in a chair or on the floor. Shake out your arms and legs, settle back, take a deep breath and close your eyes. First think of your feet and ankles. Repeat to yourself, "My feet and ankles are relaxed, my feet and ankles are relaxed." Then concentrate on your lower legs and calves, again repeating, "My lower legs and calves are relaxed". Next concentrate on your thighs and buttocks, followed by your chest, abdomen and back, then your arms and shoulders, neck and head. When you are finished, you should be completely relaxed and tension free. Get into the habit of using progressive muscle relaxation every time you feel stressed.

D. Visualization. Through visualization you can give your body and mind a well-deserved break. When you feel stress and tension building, think of a place where you feel safe, comfortable and happy. Many people think of a sunny beach in the Caribbean with warm temperatures and blue water lapping onto the shore. Whatever your visualization, begin with a deep breath, inhale slowly, hold for a few seconds and then exhale through your mouth. Visualize your special place. See the colors. Hear the sounds, Feel the warmth. Now feel your tension and stress slipping away.

Often the determination of whether something is good or bad can be in the eye of the beholder. When facing a stressful challenge or change, talk to a friend or family member. Share your concerns and ask for their thoughts and suggestions on how to handle the situation. Your support network can supply you with sympathy, understanding, objectivity, knowledge and encouragement. Remember, you are not alone. Your friends and family are there to support and help you. Don't be afraid to ask for assistance just as you would be willing to assist someone needing help.

EXERCISE 13

List your personal signs of stress (i.e. headaches, upset stomach, nervousness, inability to concentrate) and what you can do to reduce or eliminate your stress.

Signs of Stress	Actions to Reduce or Eliminate
_____	_____
_____	_____
_____	_____
_____	_____
_____	_____
_____	_____

Making the transition from work to retirement involves sharp and abrupt changes. What is expected of you and what do you expect of yourself? People who are unable to let go of the role provided by their work may find it difficult to enjoy their retirement years. There will be changes but obviously, the fewer changes in the overall pattern of your current life, the easier and more successful your adaptation will be to retirement.

Any changes you make should be gradual rather than dramatic. Your retirement activities should be introduced over time, to minimize your stress and sense of crisis. However, you don't want to make your retirement changes too slowly as you risk losing momentum and interest. Moderation is key!

The more active you are in your retirement planning, the greater your satisfaction will be with the outcome and in turn, the better your results for an increased mental attitude. By creating a retirement plan that keeps in mind the excitement and rewards ahead, you create within yourself an enthusiasm of what's to come. However, there may be times when you have negative feelings or you just feel down. In times of change, this is normal and you need to have a plan to deal with these down periods. To a large extent you can learn to handle these periods with ease. When they occur, ask yourself, "Here's where I'm at or how I'm feeling, now what am I going to do about it?" Below are commonly reported causes of down periods and some suggested actions:

• feeling holiday blues	- plan an activity away before the holiday
• feeling sorry for me	- visit someone worse off
• dreading weekends	- increase your weekend activities
• feeling guilt over something	- talk to a confidant
• feeling guilty about reading a book or taking a nap	- tell yourself "you're worth it - it's your time and you deserve it"
• getting lonely	- make contact with friends
• getting the 'winter' blues	- engage in a winter activity (i.e. skating) or investigate light box therapy

- worried over finances   - see a financial advisor
- dislike being alone at night   - consider getting a pet
- feeling lethargic   - get more physical exercise

Armed with a plan, you can head off the negative feelings or at least minimize them when they start to arise. Your plan may be as simple as going for a walk or calling a friend for lunch. It may be talking to your spouse, partner or friend about your mood swing or completing a vigorous exercise routine. The fact you've recognized and are doing something to reduce or eliminate your down periods, will greatly help you return to normal.

Remember, the more your body and mind are exercised, the fewer down periods you will have. Getting out of a blue mood is primarily a do-it-yourself project but if you are unable to pull yourself out of an extended down period, seek professional help.

If you are feeling tired more frequently, not sleeping as well as you used to, feeling isolated and out of sorts, or are resorting to alcohol as a pick me up, contact your doctor, religious leader, senior center advisor or counselor. The ability to face issues and discuss them with knowledgeable people and loved ones is greatly preferred to avoiding the issues. Remember, millions of people have retired and many felt the same way you do. You are not alone.

Harold thought he was ready for retirement. He had a good financial plan. He felt prepared and would often say, "Retirement, bring it on!"

When Harold retired, life was great for the first two months; it was like an extended vacation. Then he began to miss the office and in particular, the praise from colleagues and manager. Even though Harold had retired from work, his need for recognition continued. He missed the accolades, started to feel blue and began to take his frustrations out on his wife. He criticized her housekeeping and grocery shopping. Each day he had one or more suggestions how she could do her household activities better. During one of Harold's 'instructional' talks, his wife emotionally said, "When I married you, I did not sign up for this. If you keep this up, then I wonder if I want to stay around!"

As a result of his wife's concern, Harold made an appointment with a counselor. After a couple of sessions, he and the counselor worked out a plan whereby Harold found an activity that gave him his needed recognition and praise. He is now volunteering with two non-profit organizations assisting them in revising their organizational structures. Both organizations are thrilled to have him as part of their team and in turn, he is receiving words of appreciation. Harold and his wife now enjoy each other's company and are looking to the future.

Before growth can occur, we must have change.

~ *Thomas D. Willhite* ~

EXERCISE 14

If and when 'down periods' occur, you need to get yourself back in balance. Brainstorm at least six things you will do when the 'blues' happen.

Things I will do when the "blues" occur:

1. _____

2. _____

3. _____

4. _____

5. _____

6. _____

Mental health is not just dealing with stress and coping with down periods. It's possessing a positive attitude, eating the right foods and exercising your brain. For peak mental functioning, proper nutrition is essential. Your needs and performance are heavily influenced by diet. Beans are high in protein and a good source of fiber, which has been shown to improve cognition. Fruits and vegetables also improve cognitive skills. Eggs are rich in choline and may slow age-related memory loss. Fish is high in Omega 3 fatty acids and in antioxidants resulting in improved brain development and maintenance. Chocolate, rich in flavanols, increases blood flow to the brain. Flavanols are also found in red wine, green tea and blueberries.

In addition, physical activity is vital for brain maintenance. Not only does exercise tone your body but it also reduces stress and contributes to the overall health of your brain. Sleep is also extremely important and it's recommended that you get between six to eight hours sleep per night.

Besides healthy eating, physical activity and sleep, there are other things you can do to assist your brain cells and increase your general mental health. They are:

• Solving brain teasers and logic problems, word games and puzzles
• Playing board games that require strategic thinking, like chess and checkers
• Doing math without a calculator
• Using your less dominant hand for common activities like brushing your teeth or moving your computer mouse
• Visualizing, spelling, pronouncing and writing words backwards
• Taking up juggling
• Learning to play a musical instrument
• Memorizing lists
• Learning a foreign language
• Reading instead of watching television

EXERCISE 15

List your ideas for enhancing your general mental health: (eating a proper diet, getting sufficient sleep, completing the crossword puzzle in your daily newspaper, etc.)

_____

_____

_____

_____

_____

_____

_____

_____

D. Spirituality

Spirituality is an important part of our health and wellbeing. Spirituality is about our existence, relationship with our self, others and the universe. It is something we experience that helps us to understand life beyond what we can see, hear and feel.

As we age, we become increasingly reflective and less concerned with material things. We are more interested in the satisfaction of life – through our creative work, religious beliefs, association with our children and grandchildren and our identification with nature. Within the experience of aging, there is often an expanded sense of time in relation to quality of life. Studies completed for groups such as the U.S. National Interfaith Conference on Aging have related happiness, morale and health to spirituality. People with less spirituality, in general, are not as happy or healthy as those with a high degree of spirituality.

Older adults often turn to spirituality and religion when they meet difficult life changing events. Our spirituality and religious beliefs give us coping patterns and skills to deal with what life throws our way. Here are some ways to increase your spirituality:

• Develop a positive sense of hope. Expect good things to happen. Assess the event faced, including its severity and implications. Determine ways to resolve or get out of the situation. Recognize negative outcomes and how to deal with them. Retain your optimism about the outcomes. Use your supportive relationships and ask for help.
• Leverage past experiences and determine how they can help resolve your current situation

- Recognize the power of prayer and use it
- Find and use your artistic abilities
- Utilize relaxation and meditation techniques

As part of your retirement plan, think about how you can increase your spirituality and religious beliefs. Remember, there will be times in your life when having a strong spiritual connection will be comforting, especially when faced with a loss of mobility, job loss, illness or death of a loved one, personal or family disaster such as bankruptcy or divorce.

Marian and her husband Blake were enjoying their retirement. Both led active lives and were looking forward to many more years of togetherness. Unfortunately, Blake was killed in an automobile accident. The shock was enormous. For several weeks, Marian was in an emotional tailspin. Throughout this time period, Marian's religious leader met with her and together they prayed and spoke about Blake's life. Though not a very religious woman, Marian found her faith provided her with an inner peace at a troubling time. She appreciates the time and insight provided by her religious leader and today has a renewed identification to her religion.

EXERCISE 16

Record your thoughts on how you can increase your spirituality and religious appreciation: (regularly read my Bible, Torah or Koran, attend religious services once a month, take nature walks, think positively).

_____

_____

_____

_____

_____

_____

_____

CHAPTER 8
DEALING WITH FEAR

By now it should be engrained in your brain - retirement is a time of great change. The adoption of a new life style, being more self-reliant, making decisions on health and wellbeing, and taking on new and different responsibilities. With such change comes a chance for fear to grow.

Fears such as:

"Will I lose my physical or mental health as I age?"
"Will I have sufficient monies to permit me to accomplish my retirement plans?"
"Will disputes or mood swings affect my relationship with my spouse and friends?"
"As a retiree, will I get the recognition I feel I deserve?"

Fears cause feelings of unease and if not addressed, can act as obstacles between you and a happy retirement. As humans, we all have fears of one sort or another. Fears help us protect ourselves, and those we love. Our fear of being robbed makes us more aware of our surroundings when in unfamiliar locations. Our fear of being involved in an automobile accident makes us drive within the speed limit, wear a seatbelt and watch for careless drivers. Our fear of falling makes us take extra precaution when walking down stairs or on ice.

However, when our fears get out of control, they can snare our actions and escalate to the point of overtaking our rational thinking. Our fears can paralyze us from trying something new. We blame others, make excuses, slow down or abort our decision-making responsibilities. We grow cynical and in general, stop making progress towards our retirement goals. To help you overcome your fears about retirement, here are some actions you can take when needed:

Stay positive. Keep reminding yourself how fortunate you are to have your health, loving family and friends and to live in a free country.

Acknowledge your strengths and ability to adapt to change. Think about the changes you have already managed successfully including surviving adolescence, getting an education, finding and proposing to 'Miss Right', buying a home, raising a family, and holding a job.

Take responsibility for your mistakes. Don't make excuses. Remind yourself that if you did not make mistakes, you would never have learned how to improve.

Share your fears with people you love and respect. By talking to others about what bothers you, you receive different perspectives and input that may help you better understand your fear.

Collaborate on important issues. For instance, if you have a fear of running out of money, talk to your financial advisor as to the validity of your fear and if need be, work together to restructure your financial portfolio.

Focus on your retirement plan. Keep asking yourself "How do I move forward to accomplish what I believe is important?"

Get professional help if your fear(s) begins to prevent you from making progress with your retirement plans.

Remember, retirement is a time of change that will continue in one form or another, for the rest of your life. It's part of life and you need to deal with it. It's also one of the most exciting times; a time for exploration, shift in focus and constant demand for new knowledge and skills. This includes finding ways to react constructively to your fears. Don't let yourself grow numb to possibilities but rather take responsibility for yourself and your situation and address your fears.

Paul retired two years ago at the age of 65. Though he was in good health, Paul was afraid he would not enjoy a healthy retirement as his father died of heart disease in his 60s. Paul also feared that he and his wife, Celia, could experience difficulty with their relationship in retirement as they have led fairly separate lives. To address his fears, Paul listed the reasons for his health concerns and made an appointment with his doctor. This resulted in a full physical examination including a visit with a cardiologist. As a result, Paul received a clean bill of health, which went a long way to alleviate his concerns. Paul and Celia talked about their privacy needs and together drafted a plan regarding time together. Paul is now feeling much more at ease and his retirement fears have abated.

EXERCISE 17

List your fears about retirement	Actions you plan to take
being valued	helping the less fortunate
spending time alone	meeting 'buddies' for coffee

CHAPTER 9
HOW TO BE A SUCCESSFUL
TIME MANAGER

One of the most common complaints of retirees is not being aware of where the time goes. Often a retired person has the greatest intentions to accomplish a number of goals and activities, but the days and weeks seem to disappear without much progress. This time trap of seeming to be busy without results, can leave a retiree frustrated and annoyed.

Time management is important at all stages of life and especially in retirement. Without the skill set to manage time efficiently, even the greatest retirement plan can fail if you fritter your time away. All your best intentions will be lost and you will not accomplish your goals. So why is it we delay taking action? - Procrastination! Sometimes we put off starting something because of our fear of failure or the uncertainty of our abilities. And if we find the task tough to start, we postpone it altogether.

Leverage the management and scheduling skills you gained from your employment years. Adapt them to retirement and we are sure you'll find that at least part of what you did before to manage time will work for you in retirement.

In addition to being proactive, the following steps will help you make progress towards your goals and you, a better time manager.

Step 1

Clarify your retirement plan. Ensure your entire plan is in writing; review it and set priorities. Identify the most important part of your plan and assign it priority number one. Identify your second most important and assign it as number two. Keep going through your list until each of your goals has been ranked. Remember, this your retirement - make sure you're getting what you really want out of it. If your number one priority is to build a more loving relationship with your partner, children or grandchildren, then make sure it is at the top of your list. If making additional retirement monies is your number one priority, list it first. Failing to be honest with your plan will only lead to dissatisfaction with your results. The only one judging this is you.

Step 2

Focus on your priorities, not on your activities. Your most important priorities are those that help you accomplish your retirement plan. Keep your priorities visible. Post them on your refrigerator door, by the computer, on the mirror, or by your bed. Review your priorities daily to help you stay focused on what you really want in retirement. Another benefit to regular reminders is that they trigger your subconscious to find ways to achieve your priorities.

Step 3

Set at least one major objective designed to satisfy your priorities each day, and accomplish it. If you have set a priority to gain greater health, your objective is to allocate time each day for exercise. Whether it is going for a walk or playing tennis, do something that will benefit your mental and/or physical health. Active participation towards your priorities will keep you motivated. Be sure to give yourself a small reward for achieving your objective.

One of Norma's priorities is to get into better physical shape. At the end of each week, if Norma has exercised four or more times, she permits herself to have a Mars™ bar, a chocolate bar she loves. This self-rewarding provides regular feedback of the accomplishment and inspires her to continue the exercise program.

™Mars, Incorporated and its Affiliates. All Rights Reserved.

Step 4

Keep a time log. Captain Kirk did it and so should you. People often say that they just don't know where the time goes. If you have said this, then it's time you found out. Time is the only constant that is the same for everyone. It doesn't evaporate, it gets spent on things we do. If you choose to read the paper for an hour every morning that is perfectly fine as long as you know that you will spend seven of the available 168 hours in a week, reading the newspaper.

Keeping a log helps you track and understand how you spend your time. Each day, write down everything you do and the amount of time it takes. Be specific and record the time you spent napping, daydreaming, telephone interruptions, going to the store, bathroom breaks, driving to activities - don't leave anything out! This is the first step in identifying your time wasters so you can reduce them and concentrate on your more important issues and goals.

Step 5

Analyze everything. At the end of two weeks, analyze your time log. Take a good look at each activity listed and ask yourself, 'Was this a good use of my time?' You may be surprised to learn that you are watching television for 3 or 4 hours a day. Is this a good use of your time? Maybe, maybe not. It depends on your goals. If it's not, perhaps you can limit your television viewing to 2 hours a day. Your time log will help you find out what you do, when you do it and for how long.

As you review your time log, ask yourself:

• How much time did I spend on my number one priority?
• Was it a sufficient amount of time based on what I want to accomplish?
• What could I do differently to ensure I am spending sufficient time on my top priorities?

Step 6

Make a to-do list every day. Each morning or the night before make out a to-do list outlining, in order, the tasks that are essential for the day. These are your 'musts' that are to be completed before bedtime. At least one of these 'musts' should be an activity that advances one of your priorities. Your to-do list will help keep you on track as the day progresses. When developing your to-do list, be sure to leave room for the unexpected and interruptions. Post your to-do list in a conspicuous space such as your refrigerator door. Check off each item directly after you have completed it. Enjoy the satisfaction of stroking out each completed task!

Step 7

Make sure the first hour of your day is productive. Patterns of accomplishment are set in the first part of our day. If you have a habit of lounging over breakfast for an hour in the morning, your laid-back behavior will, in all likelihood, last for a good portion of the day. On the other hand, if you get busy accomplishing things on your to-do list immediately, your productive behavior is likely to continue throughout the day. By working on one of your top priorities early, you will be doing the most important task when you're at your best and therefore will do a better job.

Throughout your day ask yourself, "Is this a good use of my time right now?" By answering this question, you assign value to your time and ensure you are spending it in the best way possible.

Step 8

Develop the habit of finishing what you start. Don't jump from one thing to another, leaving a string of unfinished tasks behind you. If you start something then drop it for something else, you waste precious time and energy on starting and stopping, plus you get frustrated at your lack of progress. Stick with one project or task until it is completed and don't forget to reward yourself when you complete it.

Step 9

Take time for yourself. Allot time for dreaming, relaxing and having fun. With each day build in some 'play time' for you. One retiree said she completes her to-do list in the morning and then relaxes in the afternoon, whether it's reading a book, visiting with friends, volunteering, walking in the park or whatever her heart desires that day.

Step 10

Teach others. The secrets of time management are relatively simple. However, many people experience difficulties estimating and allocating their time. For some, they simply have not had the opportunity to learn the lessons of time management. For others, applying the techniques of good time management is challenging as they run counter to their personal habits or patterns. One of the gifts you can give others, including family members, is helping them learn the techniques of efficient time management and encouraging their practice. Your gift will assist them in controlling their time and in turn, enable them to achieve their personal goals.

When you control time, you control your life. In doing so, you will accomplish more, experience more satisfaction and feel more fulfilled. As these feelings increase, the quality of your retirement life increases. Satisfaction lies in accomplishing the things that are really important to you. This is another secret of having a successful retirement.

Barry is a newly minted retiree. In the first few weeks of his retirement, he slept until 9:30 a.m. simply because he could. He then read the morning paper, watched a couple of news shows on TV, showered and got dressed. By this time it was well after 11:30 am and half the day was gone.

Barry decided if he continued in this manner, he would not accomplish his retirement goals, which included finishing the basement in his home. He reviewed his retirement plan and reassessed his priorities. He started keeping a time log, which he analyzed each week. Barry scheduled daily objectives aimed at advancing at least one of his priorities. He drafted to-do lists, which included time estimates for each task. Out of necessity and desire, Barry became a good time manager and was well on his way to accomplishing his retirement goals. In doing so, he got tremendous satisfaction seeing the progress he had made in only a few short months.

EXERCISE 18

How will you manage your time? What tools or methods can you try that will help keep you organized and focused?

What I am going to do:

write out my long and short-term goals

make a 'to do' list every day

What I am going to try:

kick the procrastination habit

schedule time just for me

CHAPTER 10
JOURNALING

We live in a fast-paced world with tremendous convenience and we love to get things done quickly. We rush around, moving from one project to the next with little or no time to think about what we have done and how we did it. However, if we are to be successful in our retirement life, we need to take time to reflect on our actions to see what worked, what could have been done differently and plan for our next challenges. Journaling is a way to slow down and help us assess where we've been and where we are going.

Journaling is a personal description of events, thoughts, perspectives and observations. It is the written details of your journey through life, the journey into retirement, and your progress into a new way of living.

Journaling can also be an effective tool for stress management and personal growth. It is easy to do and provides an opportunity to note your dreams, purpose in life, memories and feelings. You can openly express what is important to you now and what you are grateful for.

Your first step to journaling is to purchase a book to write in or set up a journal file on your computer. If you choose to buy a book, decide between lined or blank pages. One of the most difficult aspects of journaling is not the writing itself, but committing the time to write. It's important to block off about twenty minutes each day. You may prefer to write in the morning as a way to start your day, or before bed as a way to reflect on the day's events. Don't think about what to say, just begin to write and the words will come.

As you write, don't just vent negative emotions or catalog happenings; write about good and bad feelings and your thoughts about the events. Don't worry about neatness or grammar; just get your thoughts and feelings on paper.

When keeping your retirement journal, begin with your vision and plan. Then list the progress you are making including your successes

---

and challenges. Also, note the questions you ask yourself about retirement, your memories and your experiences. Record guesses as to how your retirement plan may develop and reflections on striking moments and ideas. Note how you are doing with your retirement as compared to others, your thoughts, feelings and comments on how your retirement is unfolding.

An example of a journal entry may be:

Today I had a conversation with William who retired at the same time I did. He is still struggling with his retirement plan and has no well-thought out direction. He keeps referring back to his old job and buddies. In thinking about William, I am happy with the progress I am making. I have a vision, plan and action steps. Currently, I am searching for a mentor to help finalize my thinking. I regularly talk to my partner about our life ahead and very seldom look back. I have not forgotten my past but I am moving forward. I feel sorry for William and am hopeful I can help him.

Some of the things I need to address in the coming days and weeks are re-evaluating my circle of friends and how I can enlarge my social circle. I need to make an appointment with my financial advisor and I need to review my will. I plan to have my financial plans completed by month's end and my will redrafted within three weeks. I am feeling physically and emotionally well and am very much looking forward to the coming challenges and adventures retirement presents.

One fear I have is failing at my retirement plans. To help me over my fear, I plan to meet with my mentor at least once a month to discuss action steps that will help keep me on track.

At least once a week, read your journal entries for the previous seven days. Note the progress or lack of progress you are making towards your retirement goals. Mark areas of success and the reasons for it as well as areas you may have missed. Ask yourself how you can better progress towards your retirement goals in the coming week. When you have filled one journal book, immediately begin a second.

If you are worried someone else may read your journal, you're much more likely to censor your entries and you won't achieve the same benefits. To prevent worry and maximize journaling effectiveness, lock your journal away or hide it in a private place. If you're using a computer, file it obscurely or password-protect it so you'll feel safe when you write. For more information on journaling, visit www.en.wikipedia.org/wiki/journaling.

EXERCISE 19

As a practice entry in your journal, write a few lines outlining why you are looking forward to retirement and the subjects you wish to explore and accomplish.

A. I am looking forward to retirement because…

_____

_____

_____

_____

_____

B. The things I want to explore and accomplish when retired are…

_____

_____

_____

_____

_____

CHAPTER 11
A GIFT TO YOUR FAMILY

How many times have you wondered about your distant past? Where did your family originate? Who was your great grandfather or great grandmother? Are you related to royalty, a famous explorer or revolutionary scientist?

It is a wonderful gesture to leave a gift of family history to the ones you love. Now is the time to record your knowledge about yourself, your mother, father, brothers, sisters, aunts, uncles, cousins and other family members - to record your knowledge of each one, where you and the others were born, who you and they are or were, including occupations, hobbies and interests.

Also, list very crucial information about your family's medical history, facts which may be life saving for your children or grandchildren. It is amazing how much information each of us has about our families and how deeply this information will be treasured.

Recently I met a retiree named George. As it was Christmas time, we talked about the holidays including gifts that meant a great deal to us. George told me of a gift he was creating for his son. He hoped the gift would be one his son will remember and treasure for years to come.

George recently purchased a small voice recorder, which he carries with him and as he recalls things about his past or facts involving his family, he records his thoughts. Over the past two months, he has recorded family information, including names, birthdates, deaths, marriages and remembrances and stories he heard from his parents and family members. To date George has filled four tapes and was amazed with what he remembered at the oddest times.

For example, when driving in the country, George saw a barn. It was similar to his father's barn just outside of Regina, Saskatchewan. As he drove past, he remembered the time he and his pals got caught smoking behind the barn. He said he broke into a laugh and promptly grabbed his tape recorder and recorded the smoking incident. At the same time, he recorded other farm related stories that came to mind.

In his desire to leave his son as detailed a picture of the past as possible, George contacted several relatives to fill-in some of the blanks. George then researched his roots using websites and genealogical societies. He found his on-line detective work yielded a significant amount of information and the cost, other than his time, was little or nothing.

George found the two websites; www.ancestry.ca and www.yourfolks.com as useful starting points. He contacted the Family History Library, a non-denominational center, run by the Mormon Church in Salt Lake City, Utah for family information.

When asked what he thought his son's reaction would be to his gift, George answered, "Knowing my son, he will be thrilled!" When I walked away from my meeting with George, I felt uplifted and inspired. I thought, "What a wonderful, priceless gift. So special, unique and thoughtful."

What is going to be the gift you give to your family? Here are some topics you may wish to consider as a living memory for your loved ones:

• A listing and description of your values and beliefs
• Things learned from grandparents, parents, children, spouse and others
• What you are grateful for
• Hopes for the future
• Important events in your life and the lives your relatives
• Things you regret not doing
• Your happiest times
• Lessons learned the hard way
• The importance of religion

EXERCISE 20

Begin a genealogical recording of your family:

1. Write down as much as you know about you and your parents, sisters, brothers, aunts, uncles, cousins, grandparents, other family members. List names, years and places of birth, occupations, education, places of

residence, year of death, known illnesses and accomplishments.

2. Visit one or more genealogical websites entering your family information to begin your genealogy search.

3. Contact relatives to obtain an oral and written record of your family members.

4. Organize your family information in a format that can be 'gifted' to your loved ones (i.e. tapes, note book, scrap book).

Notes for getting started on your gift to your family:

_____

_____

_____

_____

_____

_____

_____

_____

_____

_____

_____

_____

CHAPTER 12
FINDING AND USING A RETIREMENT MENTOR

With many people retiring earlier, you may find yourself retired for 10, 15, 20, 25, 30 or more years. That's a long period of time!

As we matured, we worked, raised a family, and had many mentors along the way – our parents, family members, teachers, friends, coaches, business associates, supervisors and managers. They all showed us the way, pointing out the pitfalls in life and helped to steer us around the traps. They encouraged and praised us and they helped guide our actions.

Now you are entering one of the most challenging yet exciting times of your life. Retirement is filled with adventure, change and the unknown. Faced with this new part of your life, you can choose to jump into retirement with both feet, without any planning or discussion, or you can enter retirement fully prepared.

Presumably, by reading this book you want the most successful retirement possible. As part of your retirement preparation, consider finding and using one or more mentors to provide you with the advice and emotional support needed to be a successful retiree.

Here are some steps you can take to finding a suitable mentor.

1. First, acknowledge that it is hard to have a great retirement without help. One or more mentors can assist you in developing your retirement vision and plan. They can play the 'devil's advocate' to help hone your thinking. They can also provide you with ideas and options designed to achieve your retirement goals.

2. Ask yourself if there are one or two people in your immediate family who can serve as your mentor. You may consider a work colleague or friend, someone who already has created a successful retirement plan or who is already a retiree that you admire. Ask yourself, "Why do I consider this person to be a good potential mentor?" "What is it about

them I respect and would be appreciative of their assistance and guidance?"

3. Ask yourself, "What would make me an attractive mentee to my potential mentor?" "Do I have the desire and ability to accept advice and guidance from this person?" "Do I possess a positive attitude towards retirement?" "Would I be appreciative of assistance and willing to risk trying ideas and approaches suggested by this person?" "Can I feel comfortable and free to disclose personal stories and feelings with this person?" "Would we be able to share interests and understandings as part of the relationship building process?"

4. Once you identify one or more potential mentors, meet with them individually to discuss the potential of establishing a mentor/mentee relationship. It may be as simple as meeting once every month or two to generally discuss your retirement progress or it may be as complex as scheduling weekly or bi-weekly critiques of your retirement plan and actions.

When Donnie was approaching retirement at age 63, he knew he would benefit from having a mentor. He thought about those he knew personally who were successfully retired and approached Ryan, a friend he respected and who had retired 5 years earlier. Donnie asked for his assistance with his retirement vision and plan and in the following months, They met regularly. Ryan provided him with insight and observations on all aspects of retirement including how to build a dynamic health and wellness strategy, how to reinforce Donnie's relationship with his spouse, the questions to ask a financial advisor, the importance of having a balanced leisure life as well as many other related topics. Ryan asked questions, provided feedback, listened and gave advice that helped Donnie create a solid retirement plan that was both balanced and rewarding.

What Ryan got out of the relationship were good feelings of helping a friend succeed and a unique introspective to his own retirement. His advice was respected and, in many instances, followed. A strong bond of trust and admiration formed between Donnie and Ryan that enriched their friendship.

The secret of a good mentor/mentee relationship is for both parties to work towards building an effective and satisfying closeness. Mentoring is similar to other important relationships in life: it must be nurtured to reach its full potential.

Here are a few ways to help deepen your mentoring relationship:

• Develop an understanding of each other's background and issues
• Develop an environment of mutual admiration
• Treat each other as confidants
• Be open to your mentor's ideas and suggestions
• Help each other to focus on resolvable problems
• Develop a relationship that is meaningful and valuable for both parties

Mentoring relationships are not to be entered into lightly. They require a commitment of time and energy by both the mentor and mentee if valued, worthwhile results are to be produced. With the proper mix of dedication and caution, mentoring can immensely enrich your retirement and your life.

EXERCISE 21

A. Think about a mentor who would be best suited to your current retirement needs. List your possible mentors.

_____

_____

_____

B. List the most important benefits of a mentor to you.

_____

_____

_____

_____

C. As a mentee, how can you communicate your willingness to learn?

i.e. be open to my mentor's influence and ideas

_____

_____

_____

_____

D. How can you reward your mentor? Remember your mentor is spending time assisting you.

_____

_____

_____

_____

CHAPTER 13
YOU AS A MENTOR

As you succeed in retirement, you too may be approached to be someone's mentor. If so, the potential mentee admires what you are accomplishing in retirement to the point he or she feels they can benefit from your counsel. When this happens, seek out information about the mentee. Ensure your time will be spent wisely before agreeing to become a mentor.

The following are some basic strategies to assist you in your decision whether to become a mentor:

1. Have a plan. It is important for the mentee to have and be able to communicate a goal and plan for their retirement. The mentee has had to give previous thought to what he/she wants and some ideas how to get there. As a mentor, you can advise and encourage but you cannot create a retirement plan for someone else. If the plan is to be successful for the mentee, it has to be their own.

2. Bringing something to exchange. The potential mentee should be able to show how the mentoring relationship would benefit you too. The exchange for you may be the mentee's enthusiasm to learn and willingness to try new ideas and approaches. He or she may be able to provide you with a different perspective on aspects of retirement that would enrich your learning and retirement planning.

3. Make a good impression. When discussing a possible working relationship with a potential mentee, does the individual make good eye contact with you? Does he/she demonstrate attentive body language? Is he or she clear in their communication in terms of how questions are phrased? Does the mentee describe problems and challenges constructively without whining?

At the end of the discussion, take a few minutes to assess how you feel. Decide whether this is a good fit for you. Will the two of you be able to work well together? Do you feel comfortable with the potential mentee? Do you want to mentor this person?

If you decide to become a mentor, it could be one of the most rewarding experiences you ever have. Some reasons for considering becoming a mentor include:

- Gaining gratification in seeing others succeed and grow
- Fulfilling a general need to work with others
- Acquiring new knowledge and insights
- Enjoying a feeling of pride
- Deriving satisfaction from influencing someone
- Winning your mentee's respect
- Building a support network
- Enjoying the loyalty of the mentee

Well-functioning mentor-mentee relationships are rewarding for both people. It is an opportunity to share your insights and experience and for the mentee to flourish by exploring different approaches while remaining in control of his/her retirement.

CHAPTER 14
RELATIONSHIPS IN RETIREMENT

A friend is someone who sees through you and still enjoys the view.
~ Wilma Askinas ~

A. Social Circles:

As a species, humans are social beings. We feel most comfortable when surrounded by those who have mutual feelings of love, trust and understanding. Your family, friends and colleagues are important throughout all phases of life and retirement is the time when you need companionship most. As you adapt to your retirement, loved ones can help you through the rough patches and assist you in appreciating the good times.

Most people recognize that when they retire, relationships they have with people from work will change drastically or become a distant memory. In the beginning, many people stay in touch but as months pass, meetings and correspondence dwindle. Eventually, there are occasional thoughts but little to no interaction. In retirement, you need to forge a new path, let go of some relationships and build new ones.

To be successful socially, you need to work at keeping up with current friends and be proactive in seeking new ones. This means continually going to social events and gatherings, meeting people and sending out positive signals of interest. Take time to introduce yourself and inquire about the other person. Ask open-ended questions about their interests and hobbies and listen to their answers. If you show interest in them, in most cases they will reciprocate and a new relationship is formed. Keep adding people to your list of acquaintances and in time some may join your circle of close friends.

When Alice and her husband Ron retired, they moved from Toronto, Ontario to Charlottetown, Prince Edward Island, a province that had made a significant impact on the couple from previous vacations. Once settled in their new home, they made an extensive effort to introduce themselves to their neighbors. They joined a local church and each Sunday attended the coffee klatch held after the service. They became members of the local bridge club and several other organizations. In a short while, Alice and Ron had a new social circle of friends and felt very much at home.

As part of your relationship planning, think how you can reward those people important enough to be a part of your social circle. In addition to your spouse, family members and close friends, give serious consideration to your spiritual leader, doctor, insurance agent, financial advisor, accountant, lawyer and neighbor. Take time to let those in your circle know how much each of them means to you. Your spiritual leader provides you with guidance, your doctor, insurance agent, financial advisor, accountant and lawyer provide their professional advice and your neighbors, peace of mind when you are away and camaraderie when you're home.

Ask yourself how you can reward those in your social circle. It may be as simple as informing the person that he or she plays an important part in your life. A heartfelt 'thank you' lets them know your feelings and appreciation of their contribution. Other rewards could include treating the person to lunch every three or four months, sending a handwritten note of thanks or calling them on their birthday. Recognizing people for being in your life is a very personal gesture and how you do it will vary from person to person, relationship to relationship.

Cy is constantly rewarding those in his social circle. He recognizes the birthdays of his financial advisor, his accountant and life insurance agent. When asked why he takes the time and effort to remember their birthdays, Cy's answer is, "These people are important to me. They play a critical role in my life and help me keep my financial and personal affairs in order."

EXERCISE 22

List the people you consider part of your social circle. Outline what rewards you will give to signify their importance to you.

My Social Circle	Suitable Rewards
My dad	*call at least once a week*

B. Spousal/Partner Relations

At retirement, one relationship that often changes is with your spouse or partner. In the early and middle years of a marriage, couples normally don't spend a lot of time together. As partners, they are busy making a living, raising a family and fixing up a home. In a recent survey, it was found the average married couple spends only three or four hours a week together without the children, and that may be collapsing on the couch and watching TV.

Due to today's hectic pace, each partner tends to develop his/her own schedule and routine around their work, family and home demands. Then retirement comes and it's a time to relax and enjoy the fruits of your labor, which includes spending quality time with your partner. It's supposed to be the time when we enrich our relationship; when we do things and go places together.

However, a relationship filled with good times is not something that just happens. Like all other aspects of retirement, it requires planning and effort. As part of your plan, it's important to recognize that you and your partner have built up your own space and privacy needs. Each of you needs time to pursue your own interests, hobbies, tasks or just 'chill out alone'. One train of thought is if you were apart from your partner eight hours a day during your working days, you should plan to be apart approximately four hours a day in retirement. This enables each partner to have his/her own time and space. Be sure to talk with each other about your individual needs and agree on how those needs can be successfully fulfilled.

Frank and Amber agreed that when Frank retired he would participate in activities outside the home three mornings a week. They also agreed while Amber had the house to herself, she would indulge in her hobby – pottery. The couple agreed that twice a week, they would walk to their favorite pastry shop for coffee and once a week have a 'date night'. This arrangement has worked out well and Frank and Amber have recommended their 'time and space' plan to other retired couples.

As part of your planning, it's important for you and your spouse to identify to each other what retirement means in terms of roles and responsibilities. By doing this, you create a mini job description; it can outline dates, duties, responsibilities and authorities.

Before Dick and Anastasia began their retired life, they discussed who would be responsible for what in retirement. It was mutually decided that Dick would do the grocery shopping, snow shoveling and raking. He would make the bed each morning, prepare for dinner and several other domestic chores. As part of the division of duties, Anastasia would do the cleaning and vacuuming, washing and drying of clothes, folding and ironing. They agreed that household decorating would be done together. This sharing of responsibilities assisted Dick and Anastasia build a harmonious working relationship without one partner feeling he or she is doing the lion's share of the work.

For some couples, however, there is no prior discussion about what retirement means to them and who will take care of the numerous life tasks. This often leads to disastrous results.

Peter was a senior manager for a utility company and was used to telling others what he wanted and by when. His wife Pam was a successful advertising executive. When they retired, both looked forward to a life of relaxation, fun and spending time together in their garden. However, three months into retirement Peter began to criticize Pam's gardening techniques. He commented on her spacing of the plants, the way she waters and fertilizes, her pruning and other gardening flaws. Peter's nitpicking continued until one day, Pam got so angry she stormed out the door. Peter was shocked when told by a friend that Pam may not come back.

After several discussions with a counselor, Peter and Pam have reconciled. Peter recognized his need for control and worked at reducing it. He got a part-time job as a dog trainer and has learned not to criticize Pam's gardening skills.

The essential elements of a happy relationship are feeling valued, being appreciated and loved. When a couple lacks any one of these positive feedbacks, the relationship suffers and the partners drift apart.

Accepting the status quo slowly wears away at a couple's intimacy and bond.

Though it is easy to take each other for granted, the preparation for retirement provides you and your spouse an opportunity to assess and enhance your relationship. Are you thoughtful? Do you express appreciation? Have you a sense of fun and adventure? These traits among others, add to the quality of your relationship and the satisfaction level between you and your partner.

Don't fall into the trap of believing if your partner isn't complaining, everything must be okay. Keep the communication lines open and take time to listen to your spouse. Encourage discussion about each other's issues and concerns with the mindset of finding solutions.

If you tend to be indifferent about your appearance thinking it's not a big deal, take the time and make the effort to look good - not only when you're going out but also when lounging around the house.

To add spice to your relationship, do little romantic things such as buying flowers, sports equipment or treating your partner to lunch. Say 'thank you' to recognize what he/she does for you and your relationship. Spend quality time together and share fun activities. Relationships are like a garden. They require regular care and feeding if they are to grow and become fruitful.

EXERCISE 23

List some acts of kindness and appreciation you can do for your spouse to let him or her know how much you love them (i.e. make the coffee/tea in the morning, help with meal preparation, or wash his/her car).

Little Acts of Kindness

_____

_____

_____

_____

_____

_____

_____

C. Parenting in Retirement

Parenting in retirement can raise a whole number of issues. Once retired, you may find yourself re-examining many areas of your life including the relationship you have with your children. For many, your children are now adults running their own lives with their respective families.

Perhaps you decide you want to spend more time with your children and grandchildren as you take great pride and enjoyment from being with them. This is all well and good as long as your children support this decision. However, with most adult children, their time is precious – working, raising children, keeping a home and yard, maintaining relationships with friends and all the other aspects of daily life. If not carefully thought out, this is where a potential clash can occur. If you want to be with your children and grandchildren more often but your children don't share the same perspective, the result may be disappointment and some hard feelings.

Another potential difficulty that sometimes arises between retirees and their children is that an adult child may feel you can be called upon at a moment's notice. There's always a need for a good baby-sitter or someone to help with tasks such as painting or yard work. Beyond your time, your full-grown child may see you as a source for financial help. You have a pension, your mortgage is paid off and you have extra cash to spend on such things as clothes and sport fees for your grandchildren. They may expect you to pick up the tab at restaurants or help with their car or house payments.

To avoid many of these problems, you and your children need to have an honest discussion about what is expected from one another. Explore and understand each other's expectation and when either side wants too much, the other has the freedom to say, "Wait a minute! Let's talk". The same holds true with your spouse or partner.

As a retired couple you need to find the delicate balance where you can have strong, loving relationships with your adult-children without treading on their independence. This means respecting their space and allowing them to say, "Sorry, Mom and Dad, this is not a good time for you to come over".

You and your spouse can help each other achieve the correct balance of time and support to adult-children. Simply by discussion, one partner may feel the other tends to spend too much or too little time with the children and grandchildren and may suggest moderation.

Nora and Roger have recently retired. They have two daughters, Tracy and Heather. Tracy and her husband Steve live in town and Heather in a city 400 kilometers away. Tracy and Heather each have two small children who are very active in various activities including swimming, soccer and hockey. Time is precious as every minute is taken up with work, family and friends.

When Nora and Roger were employed with their respective companies, they regularly visited with Tracy, Steve and the kids every two or three weeks. Due to distance, the visits were less frequent with Heather and her children.

Now that Nora and Roger are retired, they suggested more frequent visits, like once or twice each week with Tracy and Steve and once every three weeks with Heather. When this plan was proposed, it was not received with enthusiasm as it meant a major disruption to their children and grandchildren's existing schedules. After some honest discussion, Nora and Roger's plan was revised to visits once every two weeks with Tracy and Steve, and once every six weeks with Heather and her family. Everyone agreed to the arrangement and to reviewing the frequency of visits regularly to ensure their workability.

EXERCISE 24

A. Regarding your children and grandchildren, list what you want in retirement. What does your partner want?

What do I want?

I day a week together

What does my partner want?

As much time as possible together

_____

_____

_____

_____

_____

_____

_____

_____

_____

_____

_____

_____

_____

_____

_____

_____

B. Answer the following questions regarding parenting and children.

1. Do we, and the children, understand each another's expectations?

2. Do any of our expectations need to be altered?

3. Are there any areas of disagreement between us, as a couple, about parenting? If so, how might these be resolved?

4. How much involvement, and what kind, do we want with our grandchildren? What needs to change to achieve this?

5. Are there any areas of disagreement between us as a couple about grand parenting? If so, how might these be resolved?

_____

_____

_____

_____

_____

_____

_____

C. Action plan

_____

_____

_____

_____

_____

_____

_____

_____

D. Step Grand parenting

In today's world, blended families are becoming increasingly common. Many become a step grandparent when either they, or their children, remarry someone who already has children.

Establishing a relationship with your step grandchildren is not easy. Sometimes the child or the child's parent doesn't accept you. Sometimes, neither of them does. If this situation presents itself, don't try to demand acceptance but rather take the long view – that the relationship needs time to form for you to be seen as a special person in their lives.

Don't push to be called 'Granddad' or 'Grandma'. You may have to accept being called by your first name or Uncle/Aunt. Further, don't reprimand the child unless there is a need for physical safety. Leave discipline to the biological grandparent or the child's parent(s).

As to the biological grandparents, recognize there is a natural bond between them and their grandchildren. Respect that bond and try to foster it rather than trying to compete with it. Don't try to outdo the biological grandparent's Christmas or birthday gifts. Rather work with your children and step grandchildren to create an atmosphere where both the child's parent and the children, accept you, your love and kindness.

EXERCISE 25

If you have step grandchildren, list the steps can you take to better build a loving relationship and at the same time respect the needs and feeling of the biological grandparents.

(I accept being called Uncle Jack. I will treat my step grandchildren in the same manner as I treat my biological grandchildren. I will spend the same amount of money on gifts for both my step grandchildren and grandchildren.)

_____

_____

_____

_____

E. Family Challenges

As you move forward into retirement, there will be uncomfortable situations. Whether it's the illness of an elderly parent, divorce amongst your children or one of them moving back home, it is vital that you and your partner recognize the importance of having a unified approach to problem solving. If you and your spouse disagree on how problems should be tackled; your divided thinking may act as a wedge between the two of you resulting in a damaged relationship.

Some of the more common family challenges are:

• The return of an adult child after a divorce
• A married child wanting to borrow large sums of money
• The serious illness of a parent
• The request for extensive babysitting

By not foreseeing and discussing potential problems, quick decisions may be made that may not be supported by the other partner. Critical decisions made in the heat of the moment may tear at your relationship as a couple. Remember this is the moment in your lives when you're looking forward to more peaceful times together.

To avoid conflict and 'split decisions', it is recommended you and your spouse play the 'What If?' game.

• What if our 26-year old daughter wants to move back in with us to save

money for a down payment on a house? What will our answer be?
- What if our married son wants to borrow money, how will we handle the situation?
- What if Mom gets seriously ill, who in the family should discuss nursing home options with her?

By talking about various likelihoods, you and your partner can determine, without actually facing the situation, the best action for all concerned. Weigh the pros and cons of each possible solution and rationally consider the merits of each before formulating an action plan. If and when the event occurs, the two of you have already worked out a strategy and can demonstrate a unified approach, which adds to your overall strength as a couple.

Nola and her husband Jerome have a 30-year-old son named Norm. He is single, has a good education, but has problems holding a job for more than 12 months. Norm finds something wrong with every job, whether it is the people, the pay, the hours, the lack of prospects and the list goes on. When Norm quits a job, he's in the habit of knocking on the door of either his older brother, or calling Nola and Jerome to put him up. Nola and Jerome are approaching retirement and are looking forward to a life of relaxation. However, there is the very real potential problem of the returning Norm.

As part of their retirement planning, Nola and Jerome discussed what they would do the next time Norm comes knocking. After discussing the options, Nola and Jerome agreed to permit Norm to stay for a maximum of 1 week with a financial assist of $500. Also, Norm would be told this is a one-time gift and that the next time he leaves a job, he is on his own and should not expect room, board or financial help. Both Nola and Jerome are satisfied with their joint decision and are now prepared to face the situation knowing they are both on the same page.

EXERCISE 26

With your spouse, list the potential problems or questions that may arise in your future. Together, determine the action you will take if and when the problems occur.

Potential Problems

Divorce of our daughter Kim

Potential Solutions

Help Kim financially for a maximum of three months

_____   _____

_____   _____

_____   _____

_____   _____

_____   _____

F. Spousal Communications

For many couples, retirement comes as quite a shock. Each partner has been wrapped up in his or her world of work, taking care of the kids and maintaining the home for years, which leaves little time for each other. Then comes retirement, the daily grind vanishes, the children are gone and there are just the two of you!

However, this extra time together means your old patterns of communications may be so shaken up that new communication behavior is required. If one or both partners feel they have been misunderstood, not been listened to, or treated with less than adequate respect, then spending more time together may strain the relationship. As part of your retirement planning, it is necessary to assess the communications with your spouse to determine if and what changes are needed. When completing your assessment, acknowledge your communication strengths but also note the areas where you need improvement.

When thinking about your communication strategy, ask yourself the following questions:

- Do I tune out when he/she says something I do not agree with or do not want to hear?
- Do I assume I know what he/she is going to say and stop listening?
- Do I form a rebuttal in my head while he/she is talking?
- Do I give the appearance of listening when I am not?
- Do I listen to only what I want to hear?
- Do I interrupt while he/she is talking?

If you answered 'yes' to two or more of the questions, then you should give consideration to changing your spousal communication style. Good communications between partners doesn't just happen, they have to be recognized and practiced. To assist in building more effective communications with your spouse, consider implementing the following guidelines:

a. Think through your message. What is it you want to say? What is the message you want your partner to hear and how should you phrase it? Many relationships are damaged by one or both partners saying things, or using words or tones without previous thought of their affect on the other.

Incorrect message: "You don't know what you're talking about."
Considered response: "I hear what you are saying and I have a different view."

Incorrect message: "This food isn't good."
Considered response: "This butter doesn't taste right to me."

Incorrect message: "Just drop the subject."
Considered response: "I don't think we're getting anywhere with this discussion. What do you say if we just leave it for an hour or two?"

b. Choose a good time to communicate. Ask your partner when would be a good time for him or her to talk. If the present time is not convenient, negotiate a better time. Remember, for two people to fully understand each other, both must have time to spend in the communication.

c. Give the other person your full attention. This means stopping what you are doing and listening. Turn off the TV, put down the newspaper, and make eye contact. Don't just listen, but listen for understanding. Hear the words and tone, read and understand the body language. Ask questions for clarification. Not only does giving full attention increase your comprehension, it tells the other person you are listening and that you care.

d. Avoid being defensive. Try to fully understand your partner's point of view. Try to see the world from his/her side. When you think you understand what they are saying, summarize your understanding and tell your partner, "From what you have said, this is what I heard. Am I right?"

e. Verbally follow your partner. Engage in listening to your partner's messages. This involves repetition of a person's last few words, the use of "um-humm", "I follow you", "I understand", "yes" and other such verbal encouragement.

f. Use open-ended dialogue and questions.
   Such as:
• Tell me more about…
• What are your ideas on…
• What would make for a win/win solution in your opinion…

Not only should you and your partner practice good communications, each of you needs to know what style of behavior is appreciated. For instance, most people have said they want to be (a) treated with respect, (b) truly listened to and understood, (c) treated with honesty and trust, (d) not to be lied to, (e) assured that the other will keep his/her promises, and (f) recognized for their maturity, intelligence and capability.

Every week or two, revisit your communication successes and determine what progress you are making in the areas for improvement. Over time, you will notice your areas of strength will be on the rise and the items for change are diminishing. When significant change has occurred, you and your spouse should reward your efforts by doing something special, such as a night out.

Prior to retirement Joe and Emily lived very busy lives. The only time they got to really discuss matters was the odd 'date night' and even then, conversation was primarily about work or the children.

Now that Joe and Emily are retired and have more time to talk to each other, they found much of their conversation skills are rusty. Joe agreed he has a habit of tuning Emily out when she says something he disagrees with. Emily admitted she forms a rebuttal in her mind while Joe is talking and that she doesn't hear all of what he is trying to say.

In an effort to make their conversation meaningful and more effective, both agreed to actively listen and elevate their communication skills. Although they now hear and understand each other, both recognize the need for continued efforts to maintain and improve their ability to communicate.

EXERCISE 27

A. Together with your partner, create a list of 'guidelines' for good communications. Brainstorm as many positive actions as possible, then choose eight to ten actions you and your partner will use regularly.

Our guidelines for good communications are:

Treat each other with respect

Be open and honest

_____

_____

_____

_____

_____

_____

_____

_____

B. Now identify one or two areas for change and develop an action plan aimed at reducing or eliminating these areas.

Areas for Change	Action Plan
I need to convey attention	*I will make and hold eye contact, ask open-ended questions, paraphrase and summarize*

_____   _____

_____   _____

_____   _____

_____   _____

_____   _____

_____   _____

_____   _____

G. Dealing with Conflict

Conflict is a part of life. Conflict between two people can result from good intentions or bad, from appropriate or inappropriate behavior, from praise or insult, from change or upset. Retirement can elicit emotions resulting from changing roles, fear of the unknown, being in each other's 'space', differences of opinions of what to do with your time, and a host of other reasons.

When differences surface, it helps to know how to identify and deal with the conflict so it is not draining or damaging to your relationship. You need to recognize your methods of dealing with conflict as well as those of your partner. Rest assured, they're likely not the same!

Dick grew up in a family where conflict and heated arguments between his parents were commonplace. Both parents would scream, yell and threaten each other with harm. In an effort to block out the yelling and shouting, Dick placed a pillow over his head and turned the radio volume as high as possible. Dick grew up hating conflict to the point he tried his best to avoid all potentially controversial situations as they reminded him of his youth.

Shortly after Dick and Colleen met, there was a realization they had different styles of handling conflict. Dick ignored conflict at all costs and Colleen always rushed for conclusion and resolution. Together they realized if their relationship was to survive and grow, both would have to respect each other's comfort levels with regards to conflict. Now when it occurs, Colleen says to Dick, "I believe we have a conflict and I would like to discuss it. I am prepared to meet with you in two hours. How does that work for you?" Dick then realizes he has two hours to avoid it, but at the end of the two hours he has to meet with his wife for discussion and resolution. This compromise satisfies both needs and continues to work for Dick and Colleen.

When faced with conflict do you and your partner have different approaches? If so, what changes do the two of you need to make. Is there a cooling off period? Is it important to your partner that you take a more assertive approach for conflict resolution? Do you need to bury your anger and address conflict in a more 'adult' way? Should you become less involved in issues and ask yourself the question, "Will this issue really matter to me tomorrow?"

One of the most useful results stemming from marital conflict is compromise. True compromise only happens when both partners come to an action or arrangement that satisfies both of their needs.

To help arrive at a compromise, both partners need to answer the following questions:

- What do we individually see as the problem?
- How do we think the original problem started?
- What would be the best outcome?
- What would be the very least we could accept?
- What are we prepared to compromise to achieve a mutually satisfactory outcome?

In many cases, by answering these questions the partners learn that they are not so far apart in their thinking after all. Usually, one has been laboring over a misunderstanding about their spouse's point of view or tempers have escalated to the point that bitter words (or no words at all) have been exchanged, which has masked the real problem.

When faced with a conflict situation, here are some proven ways to resolve it:

1. Be respectful. Without respect, the conflict will continue to fester and grow. Listen until you totally understand his or her point of view. You can achieve this by asking questions such as:

- Tell me why you feel the way you do?
- What did I do to add to the problem?
- What issue is important to you?
- What do you suggest we do to resolve this issue?

2. Clearly state your point of view. Once you fully understand the other person's views and thoughts about the issue, state your point clearly and briefly. Remember, with any conflict, there are two sides. You have a right to express your opinion, especially if you have treated your partner respectfully and tried to 'walk in his/her shoes'. Avoid using loaded words. Say what you mean and mean what you say. Disclose your thoughts and feelings. This means taking the time to describe how you view the problem and how you propose to resolve it.

3. Resolve the conflict. By treating each other with respect and trying to understand each other's point of view, the conflict moves from a situation filled with emotion to one that is a difference of thinking, which requires the attention of two 'adults' behaving rationally.

As with most conflicts, it is important to 'stage' it correctly. This means you should determine who needs to be part of the discussion and who should not be involved. With most conflicts, obviously the two conflicting partners need to be in attendance; however, children should not be present. Feel free to negotiate where the conflict discussion should take place. You and your partner may decide to go for a walk or sit in your car away from the children.

Both you and your partner also need to decide when is the best time to have the conflict discussion. It's unfair for one partner to launch into a conflict discussion when the other is focused on another matter. Both people need to have time to deal with the situation, to listen and understand each other, and to come to a resolution.

After each conflict, you and your partner need to ask yourselves separately,

- What did I learn from this conflict?
- Did I treat my partner with respect?
- Did I truly listen and understand his/her point of view?
- How badly was I hurt during this conflict?
- How badly was my partner hurt?

Answer these questions so that you can learn from each conflict and improve your personal resolution behavior. By positively increasing your conflict resolution skills, both partners feel worthy and valued.

EXERCISE 28

Answer the following questions:

1. How often do I blow up?

_____

_____

_____

2. Who receives the brunt of my emotions – the person causing the problem, a scapegoat, or the nearest person at the time of impact?

_____

_____

_____

3. Do I think before I react, or react before I think?

_____

_____

_____

4. In conflict situations with my partner, do I treat him/her with respect?

_____

_____

_____

5. Do I ask open-ended questions regarding the conflict and consider his/her feelings about it? Do I truly try to see the situation from his/her point of view?

_____

_____

_____

6. When describing my point of view, am I open with my thinking and emotions or do I gloss over my true thoughts and feelings?

_____

_____

_____

7. What can I do to improve my handling of conflicts with my partner so each of us comes away a winner?

_____

_____

_____

8. Do I take the time to analyze each conflict with regards to what I learned? What I am proud and not so proud of, and what do I need to change before the next conflict?

_____

_____

_____

_____

Notes:

_____

_____

_____

_____

_____

_____

_____

_____

_____

_____

_____

_____

_____

_____

CHAPTER 15
SEX AND THE OLDER PERSON

A. Physical Sex

Sex is an important aspect of living! Throughout our lives we all have thought, dreamt and practiced sex. It is a vital component to any vibrant relationship. Unfortunately, many retirees believe that sex is something they have to forget about, as it is meant for younger people. The good news is - nothing can be farther from the truth!

Why do older people see sex as something for the young? It's simple. Over time, we have allowed ourselves to be influenced by myths and falsehoods. For instance, one myth is that biology has established a mandatory age for sexual retirement among men. This is completely inaccurate. Some men over 90 years of age are still potent.

Age Group	% of adults still sexually active
57-64	73%
64-75	53%
75-85	26%

*Source: New England Journal of Medicine, August 23,2007; Volume: 357

Another myth is that people suffering from heart disease should not engage in sex due to the exertion of energy required. Actually, cardiac energy expenditure during a sexual climax is about equal to climbing two flights of stairs.

If you have questions about your sexually ability, see your physician. It's essential for you to appreciate the importance of sexual activity and how you can continue to enjoy this aspect of your retirement life.

Don't let others, such as your children, influence your views about sex. One of the primary oppositions to sexual freedom among seniors comes from adult children who have already accepted greater freedoms for themselves.

Even though some retired men report sexual activity is difficult due to erectile deficiency (ED) and a percentage of women suffer from lower sexual desire, most couples continue to enjoy regular intimacy. To increase your sexual prowess, stop smoking, engage in regular exercise, control your weight, drink alcohol in moderation and eat right. Not only do these steps help protect your heart and make you healthier overall, according to the Journal of Urology and the research completed by Dr. Eric Rimm, these actions will also increase your sexual drive and satisfaction.

B. Increasing the Romance

> *It's your unlimited power to care and to love that can make the biggest difference in the quality of your life.*
>
> ~ *Tony Robbins* ~

Besides physical sex, there is another aspect of love we sometimes overlook or take for granted. That aspect is enjoying the company of our partner - the romance of being together. It's a candlelight dinner, a walk in the park, holding hands, snuggling while watching television, or giving your partner a back rub. It is the ability to please your spouse by doing little things that brings you both pleasure and closeness. People wise in years have a way of making the most of this so-called second language of love. In retirement, you and your partner have the time and hopefully the inclination to participate in this incredibly romantic and fulfilling demonstration of affection.

Some ways to increase the closeness with your partner are:
- Pay attention to your spouse when he or she mentions an interest in things like books, movies, music, and theatrical productions. These can be the triggers for gift ideas at Christmas, birthdays, anniversaries or 'for no reason other than I love you' gifts
- Offer to give your partner a back rub or foot massage. Make your offer frequently and sincerely
- Leave cards, letters and/or notes expressing your love. When you call or e-mail, end the conversation or note with an "I love you"
- Regularly pamper and spoil your spouse. Make his or her coffee or tea in the morning, let your mate sleep in, offer to do one of his/her chores such as doing the dishes or washing the car
- Have your spouse's favorite music playing when he or she returns home
- When the two of you are in the company of others, make an effort to praise your spouse and how you appreciate all he or she does
- Make your spouse's favorite meal followed by you cleaning up
- Celebrate the time together with special lunches, surprise trips and date nights

"Have you the Karma Sutra in large print?"

Wake up each morning and ask yourself, "What can I do to make my spouse feel special today?" Use your imagination and vary your actions. Your spouse will thoroughly enjoy your tenderness and in all likelihood, respond in kind. With this concentration on the needs of your spouse and vice versa, it's a wonderful way to proceed through your retirement years!

Robert retired from his job at the age of 63 and his wife Helen continued working at a local insurance office. Upon his retirement, Robert agreed to do the housework, yard maintenance and grocery shopping.

When Helen returns home after a busy day, Robert ensures the house is clean and presentable. He also has ready a glass of Helen's favorite sherry and he ensures the evening meal is prepared and in the oven. Often times, Robert offers to rub Helen's back and lights one of her scented candles.

Helen very much appreciates Robert's attention and in turn, she reciprocates by making Robert's favorite breakfast and ironing his shirts on her days off. The couple enjoys providing each other with attention as it pleases the other and in turn, makes them both feel appreciated. They agree that their love for each other is increasing as they age and they are looking forward to spending the rest of their lives in each other's company.

EXERCISE 29

A. List the ways you can provide pleasure and romance to your partner. Consider physical sex and the second language of love. Be as imaginative as possible.

B. On the following page list the ways your partner can provide pleasure and romance for you.

What I can do for my partner

_____

_____

_____

_____

_____

_____

_____

_____

_____

What my partner can do for me

_____

_____

_____

_____

_____

_____

_____

_____

_____

_____

_____

_____

_____

_____

_____

just kidding... keep it even!

CHAPTER 16
HOW TO HAVE FUN

For hundreds of years, people have said that laughter is the best medicine. Laughing and having fun helps us relax. When we laugh our body produces endorphins that help cellular development and produces a feeling of wellbeing. This is not a new idea but rather one that has been pushed by the wayside in our ever-busy world. People don't allocate enough time for fun and relaxation and for some, have even forgotten how.

Now that you're entering retirement, it is important to revisit how to have fun. The dictionary definition of fun is: 'whimsical, mirth, amusement, informal'. As a successful retiree, you need to look at your world and ask how you can add more fun into your life? What are the whimsical and amusing things you and your partner can do to add fun and excitement to your lives? Maybe it's just taking time to joke around playfully or see the funny side of life as you go about your daily activities.

Obviously you can go out and buy entertainment and a good time, but here are some easy, very affordable ways to have some fun in everyday life:

A. Pay for the car behind you
When crossing a toll bridge, pay for the car behind you. Both you and the driver behind suddenly come alive. Don't be surprised if their car races to catch up with you, just so they can view their benefactor. Although the driver may leave bewildered, he/she certainly has a great story to tell.

B. Do something unexpected
Put a walkie-talkie or baby monitor inside a puppet, doll or bag and leave it in a high traffic area. As people walk by, say something fun like "You're ignoring me" or "I need a friend". Try this with family, friends and especially your grandchildren.

C. Transform a room

One of the fun things you can do with children is to transform the dining room into a fort by draping sheets over the table. You can then pile cushions under and around the table and all be in the fort for hours having a wonderfully imaginative time.

D. Take a trip to a toy store

Visit a toy store with your partner for the sole purpose of trying out the toys. You will be surprised at the amount of fun and the number of memories that spark from your visit.

E. Dress up in old clothes

Pull out some old clothes and play dress up. Remember the times when you wore those clothes and why they mean so much to you that you still haven't gotten rid of them.

F. Fill a loot bag

Fill a loot bag for your partner with things you find around the house. Make each item meaningful for the other person. Once filled, exchange bags and proceed to open and discuss each item.

G. Give anonymous and unexpected appreciation

The next time you are in a supermarket, gas station or restaurant, give a sincere thank you to the clerk or server for doing a great job and then watch his or her facial expression. Call your doctor's office to learn his/her birthday and send a card of appreciation.

H. Organize a paper airplane flying contest

With the neighborhood children or your grandchildren or both, teach them how to make paper airplanes and then have a contest on whose airplane will fly the farthest.

I. Plan a surprise picnic

Prepare a surprise picnic lunch for your partner together with a blanket laid out in the back yard or on the living room floor. Ready a bottle of his/her favorite wine and when your partner arrives home, lead him/her into the yard or living room and have a delightful lunch.

J. Give your partner a day off
One day every few weeks, tell your partner he/she has the day off to do whatever they wish and that you will do the cleaning, gardening, or whatever needs to be done. Have a delicious dinner prepared when he/she returns.

K. Remember your high school days
Pull out your high school yearbook and reminisce about your school days. Try to imagine what your classmates may look like and what their life story has become.

L. Field trips
Take a trip to a local winery, brewpub, museum, art gallery, or antique shop. Make a day of it with lunch, a walking tour of the area and a leisurely time on a park bench.

M. Play childhood games
With your spouse, brainstorm what you played as children – this will help you recall the games of your youth. Then teach your grandchildren how to play the many games you grew up with – "I Spy", "Ring-around-the-Rosie", "Battleship", "Find me!"

N. Create a laugh-a-day challenge
Challenge your partner to a laugh-a-day contest. The object is for each of you to come up with the best laugh of the day. You may use any materials you wish – newspapers, comics, cartoons, on-line jokes, skits, etc. Declare a winner at the end of the day and have a prize that can be battled for again and again.

O. Go on a photo safari
Take your camera and try to obtain the most unusual photo within your house or neighborhood.

P. Distribute stuffed animals
Buy several stuffed animals and distribute them at a local seniors home. When distributing the toys, take time to talk to the seniors. Find out something interesting about each person.

Q. Volunteer for the next Santa Claus parade

Contact the local organizer of the Santa Claus parade or any other parade of your choice, and volunteer to be a character within it. If necessary, plan and prepare your costume.

The above are only a handful of ways you can have fun. Let your imagination go wild. What would be fun to do? What are you comfortable with? Great! Now go do it!

EXERCISE 30

List some ways you and your partner can have fun. Be imaginative as possible.

_____

_____

_____

_____

_____

_____

_____

_____

_____

CHAPTER 17
INCREASING YOUR SELF-ASSERTIVENESS

You gain strength, courage, and confidence by every experience in which you really stop to look fear in the face. You are able to say to yourself, 'I have lived through this horror. I can take the next thing that comes along.' …You must do the thing you think you cannot do.

~ Eleanor Roosevelt ~

Though self-assertiveness is important at every age, its importance increases as we grow older. Being assertive gives us self-confidence and a sense of being 'in control' of our actions and lives. An assertive person acts in his or her own best interests, stands up for what they believe in, expresses feelings honestly and does it without trampling on the rights of others.

A non-assertive person usually feels anxious and susceptible to the influences and direction of others. He or she feels helpless, tends to take on everyone's problems and says 'yes' to inappropriate demands and requests. A non-assertive person allows others to choose for him or her, resulting in hurtful and potentially angry feelings about his/her inability to act.

An aggressive person wants their own way and ignores the rights and feelings of others. Aggressive people are normally angry and want to dominate.

Though each one of us has a dominant personality style - assertive, non-assertive or aggressive, we can learn to adapt to life's situations, which enables us to demonstrate assertive behaviors. Being assertive permits us to feel good about ourselves as we deal with an irritating event.

The following are examples of where an assertive behavior will help you feel more in control and may even resolve the problem outright:

A. Addressing poor service

There is no reason why you should accept anything less than what you've contracted from a service provider or tradesperson. In any transaction, it is important to have in writing a clear record of exactly what is to be done that has been agreed to before the work begins. As soon as you realize there is a problem, contact the provider/tradesperson at the work site and review your written outline. It helps if you speak early in the day and work week so the provider/tradesperson has the rest of the week to make alterations. Remember, it's important to stay calm and ensure the conversation is held in private to minimize any embarrassment in front of other trades people.

Since the only real leverage you have is financial, you should not pay until you are truly satisfied with the job. Your goal is to get the work redone without incurring any further charges. If the work is redone to your satisfaction, be willing to compromise on timing. Depending on the service provider or tradesperson's willingness to redo the work, you may consider making a partial payment. Once the alterations are made, sincerely thank him or her and pay in full.

B. Returning unwanted merchandise for a cash refund

Though most retailers are willing to accept returned merchandise in exchange for a store credit or another item, many are reluctant to give cash back. When returning an item, make sure it is in exactly the same condition as when you purchased it so there is no question that the item can be resold. In addition, make it clear that you are not interested in an exchange or store credit. You must be willing to say you need a cash refund, that the money is important and you are not in a position to accept any kind of financial loss.

Throughout the discussion with store personnel, stay calm. If necessary, ask to speak with the store manager or other person in authority.

C. Appealing a bureaucratic decision

Bureaucratic decisions are normally made following set rules, regulations, policies and procedures. When dealing with a decision you take offence to, begin working your way up the bureaucratic ladder until you reach the executive level.

As you progress, be polite and compliment everyone you speak with. Insist on your right to present your argument and to appeal decisions. Always get names and use them so as to personalize the exchange. Realize your final leverage is pursuing matters legally. As with all assertive actions, remain calm and friendly. If you are offered a compromise settlement, negotiate and accept.

D. Returning a meal in a restaurant

If you don't like a dish or the meal was not prepared to your liking, immediately call the waiter over and quietly give a specific reason for your dissatisfaction, "My meal is cold", "My meat was not cooked as ordered", "My dinner is too spicy for me". In most instances, your request will be acted upon without any further ado. However, if in a restaurant where the waiter is not empowered to accept returns, ask to speak with the chef or maitre d'. If the chef or maitre d' doesn't respond, politely make your dissatisfaction clear in a voice loud enough for surrounding diners to hear.

E. Asking for a lower interest rate on a credit card

Lower interest rates on credit cards are possible. Most banks have more than one rate and are willing to waive annual fees for preferred customers. Speak with someone at the managerial level of your bank. Remember, this is a straightforward business discussion. State your request openly and honestly without threats of taking your business elsewhere. If you do not receive the appropriate action on your request, think about canceling your card or changing banking institutions. Once you have firmly decided to cancel your card or change banks, ask to speak with the banking representative and present your decision. If there is no action by the bank to keep your business, follow through with your decision and cancel or change.

In almost every situation you face whether it is complaining about poor service, returning an item to a store, voicing your displeasure about a meal or asking for a lower credit rate, there is an advantage to having the last word. This means expressing thanks for getting what you asked for, asking for reconsideration of a rejection, requesting another meeting or saying you will call back. Having the last word helps you retain control and allows you flexibility for future action.

In any assertive action, it is important to stay calm, listen to the other party and suggest alternatives so that both parties feel satisfied. The moment you get angry or belligerent, you lose. If the other party gets angry, either absorb their comments or deflect them, but do not respond in kind.

After each assertive situation, ask yourself,
• What am I proud of in how I handled this situation?
• What am I not so proud about?
• What will I do differently the next time around?

Evaluation helps to hone your skills to the point where being assertive in tough situations will come naturally.

Harold is fifty-nine years old and a successful manager with a large utility company. Though assertive at work, he has difficulty being assertive with trades people, gas station attendants, store clerks, restaurant waiters and others outside his job. Harold used to accept poor service without saying anything. Though he was furious on the inside, outwardly Harold did nothing. One day a friend commented on Harold's non-assertive behavior and suggested he assert himself. Harold's friend demonstrated how to ask for what is wanted. His friend convinced him he would feel better about himself.

Harold's first test of his newly acquired assertiveness skills came when he approached a carwash attendant to point out the ineffective job the wash did on his car. The attendant made excuses including stating the style of Harold's car prevents it from receiving a thorough wash.

Throughout the exchange Harold calmed repeated his car was not clean. After a few minutes, the attendant offered to either rewash the car or refund Harold his money. Harold decided to take his money and drove off with a satisfied smile. He felt good that he had not been "ripped off" and satisfied on how he had calmly and assertively, stood his ground.

EXERCISE 31

A. Take a moment to think about yourself. Are you naturally assertive, non-assertive or aggressive? What were the factors that led to your "assertiveness", "non-assertiveness" or "aggressiveness"?

_____

_____

_____

_____

_____

_____

B. What can you do to improve your assertiveness? (i.e. Calmly repeating what you want over and over like a broken record, letting criticism roll off your back, stand up for your rights)

_____

_____

_____

_____

_____

_____

CHAPTER 18
CHOOSING WHERE TO LIVE

Where will you live when you retire?

Most retirees decide their current home meets their retirement needs. They like the neighborhood and want to stay close to friends, children and grandchildren. In their residence, they are comfortable and they like the climate. It has the advantage of being near medical facilities, known professionals and it is where they feel safe and secure.

However, a small percentage of pre-retirement people and retirees decide to move. Some may choose a warmer climate, the cottage or a smaller home. Others want to be nearer to family and friends, which may mean moving back to their country of origin.

If you are contemplating a move to a different time zone or geographical location, make sure the advantages outweigh the disadvantages. Don't be influenced by others when making your decision. If you have concerns about the potential destination, take some time and do research. You and your partner may consider taking an extended holiday, including renting in or visiting the new location at different times of year. Give yourself the opportunity to review all factors of your move before making the leap. Remember, this is your time and it's your decision when, where and if, you move.

To guide you in your decision, consider the following questions:

1. Will the new climate enhance my/our life and living?
2. Is it less demanding with less chance of illness?
3. From a cost point of view, will the new location reduce our utility bill?
4. Are the available properties in the area within our means to buy or rent?
5. Will we require less or different clothing?
6. Does the geographical area fit our way of life? If you are used to the changing seasons, will the area provide that pleasure?

---

7. Will we fit in with the local social scene?

8. Will it be easy to meet and make new friends?

9. What would it cost to move there?

10. What is the tax structure like? provincial, state and local taxes?

11. Are our favorite leisure activities available? How do their costs relate to what we are used to paying/able to afford?

12. Are medical facilities easily accessible? Are they able to treat our specific health problems?

13. Would our present medical plan be recognized?

14. Are physicians available and taking patients?

15. Is adequate public transportation available?

16. Are family and friends close by?

17. Will we be happy in this location 5, 10, 15 years from now?

18. Do both my partner and I really want to move there?

Notes:

_____

_____

_____

_____

_____

_____

_____

_____

_____

_____

Raymond and his wife Helen moved to Florida shortly after Raymond retired. The decision to move was influenced by some friends who continually spoke of the sand, sea and casual way of life in the 'sunny south'. Their friends painted a rosy picture of life in Florida.

In the years leading up to retirement, Raymond became an avid curler and was passionate about the sport. He looked forward to the two times a week that he played and thoroughly enjoyed the camaraderie of his curling buddies.

Several weeks after Raymond and Helen sold their house and made the move, Raymond had the urge to curl. However, to Raymond's surprise, there was very little recognition of the game in Florida and literally no demand for curling facilities. Raymond was devastated and longed for his old home and curling buddies back in Canada.

If you are thinking of selling your home and moving to a condominium, retirement centre, recreation complex or purchasing a trailer, you need to thoroughly explore whether your move or purchase is right for you and your spouse.

Harry and Paula had a dream of touring North America with a truck and trailer. When Harry retired, the couple sold their home of 30 years, purchased a 20-foot trailer and hit the road. For the first couple of weeks, it was like a honeymoon – no worries, just the open road. After a while, both Harry and Paula, who were used to their privacy, found the trailer living space to be confining. They seemed to be in each other's way with nowhere to 'escape'. This led to frequent complaints about tiny living space and heated arguments over trivial things. After two months of cramped living and numerous harsh words, Harry and Paula sold the trailer and bought a house in a small Ontario community. Their relationship got back on track and to this day, both are much happier.

In retrospect, Harry and Paula agreed they should have rented a truck and trailer for a couple of months before selling their home. This would have provided them with the experience of trailer living, including the confined quarters prior to making any major decisions.

Whatever you decide about your living arrangements or locations in retirement, choose carefully. Of course all decisions can be changed but you will not likely be able to return to your old way of life at your previous address. My recommendation is to rent, travel and enjoy. Then decide. After some time away you may just realize there is no place like home.

For information about cottages, condos, trailers or retirement communities, log-on to: www.condominiums.com, www.onlycottage.com, www.gorving.com, and www.topretirements.com.

If you do decide to move be sure to take your positive attitude with you. Also, within reason, take your prized possessions. Once you get settled, be sure to engage in a number of local social activities to meet new people and establish your social support system. The people you interact with will be instrumental in making your new home a happy one.

EXERCISE 32

List the advantages and disadvantages of moving:

1. Staying where I am:

Advantages

I love my home

_____

_____

_____

_____

_____

Disadvantages

Home ownership is expensive

_____

_____

_____

_____

_____

2. Renting:

Advantages

No maintenance problems

_____

_____

_____

Disadvantages

Rent increases

_____

_____

_____

3. Moving to a condo:

Advantages

Usually safer than a private home

_____

_____

_____

Disadvantages

Rules to follow, association involvement

_____

_____

_____

4. Buying a mobile home:

Advantages

Less capital investment

_____

_____

_____

Disadvantages

Neighbors too close

_____

_____

_____

5. Retirement Center:

Advantages

Offers greater protection

_____

_____

_____

_____

Disadvantages

Fewer younger people around

_____

_____

_____

_____

6. Move to the cottage:

Advantages

Close to nature

_____

_____

_____

_____

Disadvantages

Away from needed medical facilities

_____

_____

_____

_____

7. Settle in a warm climate:

Advantages

Don't have to shovel snow

_____

_____

_____

_____

Disadvantages

Not regularly seeing grandchildren

_____

_____

_____

_____

A. Downsizing

Downsizing to a smaller home in your present community may be a positive and practical choice to living a simpler life. The exchange of a 'big' house that feels empty for a home with the right amount of space, may be appealing as the new home will be easier and less time-consuming and hopefully, less expensive to maintain.

If you do decide to downsize, don't try to take all your current possessions and stuff them into your new, smaller home. Right size before you move! Examine your furniture and other goods with a critical eye. Make your decisions with the big pieces first.

With each piece of furniture, ask yourself:
• Do we still like it?
• Does it add value to our life?
• Will we use it regularly?
• Does it work with the existing or desired décor in the new house?
• Is there space for it?

Now is the time to unload other people's articles, including things you have stored for your children, to their rightful owners. Have a garage sale; make donations to a charity or organization to help lighten the load. Don't get stuck moving unneeded items because if you do, your smaller home will soon feel like Harry and Paula's trailer - cramped and confining.

CHAPTER 19
CARING FOR PARENTS

Building on what was discussed in "Choosing Where to Live" is the potential need of caring for an aging parent and all the questions that go along with it. Can you get them help at home? If so, how do you go about doing that? Do they need to go into a retirement or nursing home? What about your home? Do you have enough space and more importantly, do you and your partner want them moving in with you?

I. Home Care

There may come a time in your retired life that your or your partner's parents are no longer able to live a happy, safe and healthy lifestyle in their place of residence. Depending on your family circumstances, you may be the one faced with the task of obtaining care for them. When accepting this challenge, take time to find the most suitable person who will assist with the care and comfort of your loved one. Here are steps to finding the right candidate:

Step 1

Advertise. A sample ad could read as follows: "Female needed part-time for personal care and housekeeping for older disabled woman. Flexible hours. Call 416-555-1234 after 7:00 pm."

Step 2

Screen candidates. Before arranging an interview, create a job description and make sure to ask a few questions so that the person applying understands the basic duties and schedule. This will give you insight into the prospective employee's experience and training. In addition, be ready to provide information such as:

• How many hours of work are needed (total per week or month)
• What days and times are needed

- Specific duties including driving, if applicable
- Salary and benefits, frequency of pay
- Other specifics (e.g. non-smoker, must speak fluent English)

Step 3

Interview candidates. Interviewing is key in your hiring process. This is where you ask detailed questions and begin to evaluate which candidate is best suited for the job. Use the following questions as your guide:
- Tell me a little about yourself, your interests and hobbies.
- How do you feel about working with an elderly or disabled person?
- Where have you worked before? Do you have experience working with an elderly or disabled person?
- Do you know about _____ ? (ask about relevant illness or condition)
- Do you have any health or physical problems that might hinder you on the job? (ask about lifting, bending, ability to drive, etc.)
- What other obligations do you have (i.e. school, part-time job) that will affect your schedule?
- Do you have your own car? Would you be able to transport someone in a wheel chair?
- How do you handle someone who is upset, angry or fearful?
- What made you choose this kind of work?
- How do you feel about smoking, drinking or using drugs?
- Is there anything in the job description that you would not do?
- Do you have any questions about the job duties, schedule or salary?
- Is there anything else you would like to add?
- Please give me two work-related references and one personal reference.

Step 4

Evaluate the candidate. After interviewing a candidate, take time to note down your impressions, concerns and gut feelings. Try to do this immediately so the person is still fresh in your mind. Ask yourself:

- Did the person arrive on time?
- Did I have a good feeling about the person?
- Did we agree on the duties and schedule?
- Did the person provide the requested references?
- Did I tell the person when I would notify her?
- Was there anything about the person that made me uncomfortable?

Step 5

Check references. Once you have narrowed your choices, be sure to check the background of each candidate. Use the following questions to check with prior employers.

- How long have you known the candidate?
- What was his/her position?
- Tell me about the responsibilities of the job.
- What is your impression of him/her as a worker?
- Is the person reliable? Punctual?
- Did the candidate show initiative or wait to be told what to do?
- Does the person listen well? Follow instructions?
- Is the person trustworthy?
- Does she show good common sense?
- Were there any problems on the job?
- Were you aware of any problems with drugs or alcohol?
- Would you recommend this person?

Step 6

Select the candidate and offer the position. Hiring a home care worker requires patience and trust, and your instincts will be important. The time invested in screening candidates and checking references will greatly improve your chances of finding someone whose qualifications meet your care giving needs.

Once hired, ensure your home care worker has all the critical information and documentation that may be needed in an emergency such as:

- Name and contact information of your parent's family doctor
- Health card number
- List of allergies
- List of medications
- Medical history
- Name and contact information of next of kin (home, work and cell numbers)
- Name and contact information of the substitute decision maker – an individual appointed to make decisions should your parent be deemed incapable – or attorney for personal care
- Contact information for the Power of Attorney (a legal document that gives someone the right to act on your parent's behalf in financial matters)

II. Nursing Home Care

Another possible situation is finding a nursing home for a parent who is no longer able to live on his/her own. Prior to making your decision, take the time to investigate the nursing homes available to determine the best facility given the finances and the need for comfort and service, for your loved one. Use the following to assist you with your review of homes:

- Note the type and location of nursing home alternatives.
- Are private and semi-private accommodations available?
- Do they have long-term care?
- What facilities are offered? (i.e. recreation, lounge, dining room)
- Check the staffing levels including Registered Nurses and Certified Nursing Assistants
- What equipment is available? (i.e. adjustable beds and chairs)
- Check quality measures and standards
- What are the visiting privileges?
- Are safety plans including fire evacuation procedures adequate?
- Is a doctor available day and night?
- Does the nursing home offer moving assistance?

Prior to deciding on a nursing home, check the home ownership. Is it run by an independent non-profit organization or a private company? Non-profits may offer more one-on-one care than private operations. Talk to the home administrator about quality standards, inspections and turnover of top-level staff members. Visit each home several times at different hours including day and night. Is there a discernable difference in what you see at various times?

III. Parents Moving In

Another option when determining care for a parent is to have them live with you. Before making this decision, survey your home as to the feasibility of renovating. Would you need a self-contained suite or an additional bedroom? Does your property have enough space for an addition and what are the construction bylaws in your area? Consider the needs of your parent. Will climbing stairs be a problem? Is your basement suitable for a suite?

It's important to recognize the costs associated with making renovations. According to Rob Dover of Rock Solid Installations, costs for converting a basement into a fully contained suite may be as high as $50,000. A 500 square foot addition is in the neighborhood of $85,000 and adding a single 150 square foot room to a house can be upwards of $10,000 to $15,000.

Even if your parent has no trouble with mobility now, think about their future needs. Things such as:

• Widened doorways to accommodate wheelchairs or walkers
• Levers instead of doorknobs to make opening doors easier
• Grab bars in bathrooms
• Showers instead of tubs for ease of access
• Enhanced lighting, especially in stairways, kitchens and bathrooms
• Minimal stairs and level changes
• Stairs with closed risers
• Sturdy handrails
• Raised toilet seats for easier access

As part of your deliberations, you and your spouse should discuss what costs are to be shared with your parent and which are your parent's responsibility. As an example, if you build a self-contained suite, how much money would you expect your parent to contribute to the cost?

Once occupying the suite, would you expect them to pay for their own groceries, telephone and cable? Do you expect them to share the costs of heat, electricity, water and taxes?

The decision to hire a home care worker, place a loved one into a nursing home or have a parent come live with you, is not an easy one. The more you and your spouse discuss the options in an open and trusting way, the better the decision and its acceptance. Include your parent in the discussions and get his/her suggestions. Try not to make such an important decision quickly or emotionally. Give yourself time to reflect on the possibilities and outcomes. Be sure to consult with family members and knowledgeable community advisers before making your final decision. For further information, visit www.cdnhomecare.ca or www.usahomecare.net

Jan's elderly father lives alone. At the present time he is able to do his housekeeping, shopping and gardening. Recently, he has fallen several times resulting in short stays in hospital. His eyesight is also failing and his arthritis is making him less agile. Jan and her husband Nick know it will not be long before some action will be needed.

Jan and Nick have explored the options of keeping her father in his current residence, moving him to a nursing home or having Jan's father live with them. After discussing the situation, they both agreed to hire a housekeeper for Jan's father for the first year. They would then convert a part of their home into a self-contained suite providing privacy for Jan's dad and an opportunity for them to assist when needed. Prior to making this decision, Jan and Nick consulted with Jan's father who agreed it was the best alternative.

EXERCISE 33

Considering the age and health of your parents, what actions do you envision occurring in the next five years? Will your parents or spouse's parents be able to live on their own or will homecare or nursing care be required? Would or could you and your spouse have a parent share your home?

Notes:

_____

_____

_____

_____

_____

_____

_____

_____

_____

_____

_____

_____

_____

_____

CHAPTER 20
MAKING A WILL

You might be surprised how many people die each year without a will. There are numerous reasons for this major oversight including; those who cannot or will not think about death, those who believe talking about and creating a will may cause problems with their partner or family members, and those who don't want to spend money on lawyers.

If you die without a will, the province or state in which you live will decide how to distribute your estate. Each provincial or state government has its own common and impersonal formulas for the distribution of your assets. Some money or belongings may not end up with the beneficiaries you intended. For example, under provincial/state laws, each child receives a proportion of your estate regardless of need. As well, without a will, there could be no special gifts to a lifelong friend or bequest to your favorite charity.

Having a proper will goes a long way to prevent family arguments. The guesswork is eliminated and the family is clear on your intentions. Furthermore, a will may actually save money because without one, the provincial/state authorities are in control and that could mean unnecessary delays and extra costs.

It is not only important to prepare a will, but once you have one, it should be reviewed every two or three years to ensure it is still in line with your wishes. In today's world with blended families resulting from divorce and remarriage, changing financial and property accumulation, an up-to-date will is essential.

When preparing your will, it is strongly recommended you use the services of a lawyer. Don't try to do it yourself. Before consulting with a lawyer, sit down and map out exactly what your estate consists of and how you want it divided. This action will help you sort out your options and will save time and money when meeting with your lawyer.

A. Naming an Executor

As part of your estate planning, give special consideration to naming an executor. Your executor acts as your estate's legal representative. The normal responsibilities of an executor is as follows:

- Locating your original will and documents amending your will
- Confirming with your lawyer that it is valid
- Securing inventories and appraise your valuables and assets
- Participating in your funeral arrangements and if necessary, notifying your next of kin
- Protecting your property including the continuation of fire and theft coverage
- Hiring a lawyer to obtain probate, if necessary
- Identifying debts, pays all bills, taxes and creditors
- Getting investment, legal, business and tax advice
- Distributing your assets according to your wishes, to your beneficiaries

When choosing an executor, consider the following:

1. Choose a family member if possible. Family members are normally motivated to work quickly and some will do so without a fee. By law, executors are entitled to collect up to 5% of your estate for their time and effort.

2. Assess your particular needs. Do you operate a business; have substantial investments or rental properties? If so, you may need an executor with special skills.

3. Consider your long and short-term goals. The execution of most estates can be completed in less than one year. However, if you have a disabled beneficiary, you may need to protect his/her inheritance on a long-term basis. This may require an executor who is prepared to undertake the role for a lengthy period of time.

4. Avoid conflicts of interest. Don't try to patch up family feuds by forcing relatives to work together as executors and don't ask your financial advisor to be your executor as he/she may be in a conflict of interest.

5. Name a back-up executor. Give consideration to naming a back-up executor who would take the place of your executor if for some reason, your originally named executor cannot fulfill his or her duties.

6. Ask for consent in advance. Before you invest time with your lawyer preparing your will, get your proposed executor's verbal consent. Professional executors, such as a trust manager, will normally consent in writing and at the same time, confirm the fees to be charged.

B. Accompanying Letter:

It is recommended you draft a letter to accompany your will. The letter should include the following:

1. People to be notified at the time of your death

Certain people and institutions need to be notified of your death including your lawyer, executor, trustee and accountant, along with Federal pension authorities. Relatives and special friends will want to know as soon as possible so providing names, addresses and telephone numbers will make it easier for the person assuming this responsibility. Relatives and friends can provide emotional support to your spouse and family.

2. Listing advanced funeral arrangements

Be sure to communicate your funeral arrangements and last wishes (i.e. body burial, type of casket, cremation, and hymn requests). Include a reminder that the funeral director is to provide multiple copies of your death certificate needed for processing insurance and pension claims.

3. Location of personal papers

Give the exact location of your personal documents. These include birth and marriage certificates, diplomas, military papers, etc. It's a good idea to gather your documents and store them in a single location.

4. Listing of bank accounts and bank locations

List all bank accounts by name of institution, branch address and type of account. Also give the location of cancelled checks and bank statements along with the number and location of your safety deposit box and key.

5. Listing of credit cards

List by issuer and card number. If there is an outstanding balance, ask that these accounts be paid immediately and the cards destroyed.

6. Location of deed and mortgage papers

Indicate where your deeds and mortgage papers are located and when mortgage payments are due. Note the renewal date and institution holding your mortgage.

7. Listing of insurance policies

List all life, auto, home, veterans', medical and other insurance policies. Name the agent(s) and give the location of these documents. Describe any loans you may have taken out against any of your policies.

8. Listing of vehicles

List where the registration and other papers are to be found for all vehicles and boats you own. Provide the location of all keys and operating instructions.

9. Income and property taxes paid and owing

Provide the location of your income tax returns for the past three years. Record property tax amounts and due dates. Name your tax advisor and any special instructions.

10. Investments including mutual funds, stocks and bonds

List all stocks, bonds, certificates of deposit and other investments. Indicate the location of your investments and the name and address of your financial advisor. If you have any gold or silver coins or bars, provide the location and details.

11. Listing and location of valuables

List all jewelry and other valuables (i.e. china, glassware, art, etc.). Your list may also include the names of those to whom the articles are to be given.

12. Trusts, loans, money owed to you

List any trusts you have established and provide the name and address of the trustee. Record all loans and other accounts payable. Give full information on the terms and payments. List all debts and other loans owed to you. Be as descriptive as possible.

13. Special survivor benefits

List all possible sources of benefits not named in your will – government pension, veterans pension, employee pension, fraternal associations, etc.

With a current will and accompanying letter of assets, document location and burial wishes, you will feel more at ease that your final plans will be fulfilled. Let one or two family members know where your will and accompanying letter are stored and the name and address of your lawyer. Better yet, give a copy of your accompanying letter to your spouse, a trusted friend and/or family member so when you do pass away, they can begin the process of notifying your family and friends and fulfilling your wishes.

Gabrielle did not want to burden her family with undue hardship when she passed on. She wanted to make the settlement of her affairs as easy as possible. Gabrielle updated her will every three years at which time she reviewed and modified the contents of her accompanying letter. She provided a best friend with a copy of her will and accompanying letter.

Though Gabrielle isn't planning to leave this earth anytime soon, she has the peace of mind that her last wishes will be followed. She also knows her family and friends will not be put through the anguish of trying to locate her personal papers and documents at a time that will be difficult enough.

EXERCISE 34

In the following space or on a separate piece of paper,

1. Name your executor and reasons for your choice.

_____

_____

_____

_____

2. Using the points listed above, prepare your accompanying letter beginning with a listing of people to be notified when you die.

_____

_____

_____

_____

_____

_____

_____

_____

_____

_____

_____

3. If this is not a first marriage for you, how are your legal issues different from those of original-marriage couples? What are your wishes?

_____

_____

_____

_____

4. If you are in a committed but unmarried union, what have you and your partner done to protect each other legally? What more should you do?

_____

_____

_____

_____

5. Keep your information in a safe place until you see your lawyer. At the meeting, review the information with your lawyer.

_____

_____

_____

_____

Notes:

DON'T JUST RETIRE - *LIVE IT, LOVE IT!*

CHAPTER 21
THE DEATH OF A SPOUSE OR FRIEND

We all like to imagine retirement as a time we will enjoy to the fullest by doing whatever it is we want to do. While this is true, it is also a time when we could face the death of a loved one. This can be one of life's most painful and frightening situations. Not only do you suffer from a broken heart, you may now have to face the future alone. At that moment, you could be emotionally vulnerable and desperately in need of support.

People deal with death in very different ways. Regardless of your methods, you will likely need some help to cope in your time of loss. The support of family and friends provides necessary sympathy, patience and understanding. It takes time to heal and the length and intensity of the grieving period depends largely upon the situation and the individual. Remember, grieving is not a weakness; it is a necessity.

The Stages of Grieving:

1. Denial – at this stage you have trouble believing your loved one is truly gone. Denial is a cushion in your mind that helps you get through this difficult time. Don't rush or bulldoze your way through this stage. Denial, as with all stages, will end when you are ready. Let it happen gradually. This stage may last for several weeks or several months.

2. Anger – you may be angry about your spouse's departure from your life. It is a common feeling and it is natural. Anger helps you move towards regaining control of your life.

3. Bargaining – this is the stage when you ask the "what if" questions. "What would have happened if I had done more for him or her?" "What if I had been more supportive?" Don't beat yourself up about the past. What's done is done and it cannot be changed.

4. Resignation – in this stage you start to accept reality. You begin to get balance back in your life and you can start looking forward.

Obviously, there will still be lows but they will be more in balance with the highs.

5. Acceptance – you truly accept the passing of your loved one. You begin to review your options and make decisions about the rest of your life.

During the grieving process, give yourself time to heal. Don't make any major decisions such as moving, changing jobs or remarrying for at least six months to one year. You need time to learn who you are without your spouse, and how to live with and by yourself. Although difficult, it is an incredible time of self-discovery.

Throughout the grieving process, keep in touch with friends and family. Share your plans, dreams, fears and apprehensions with them. Allow yourself to feel sadness, anger and other emotions. Find a way to express your feelings through talking, crying, ranting, or whatever else works for you. Attend religious services regularly as faith can act as an anchor in your time of need. Take care of your physical health and be aware of any signs of stress or illness. Speak with your doctor if you feel your grief is affecting your health.

Just as you are feeling grief, others are too. Help and support them in their grieving. Offer support to family members and friends. Be honest with your children and grandchildren about what has happened and about how you feel. Encourage them to talk about their feelings. As your sense of grief becomes less intense, start to pick up the pieces. Return to your interests and activities and start to make a new beginning. Remember, life is unpredictable and the more you take care of yourself, the easier it will be for you to get through this difficult period.

When you lose a spouse, you may choose to connect with a widow/widower support group. Information can be obtained by contacting a community organization such as the Canadian Mental Health Association or National Mental Health Association, which can help you find the support you need.

From a practical point of view, there are some issues you will need to deal with:

A. Financial considerations: Check with your spouse's bank to determine if you have access to account balances for immediate needs. Also contact your spouse's employer regarding benefits paid to you. Consult with your financial advisor as to your situation and where else you can turn for funds.

B. Funeral arrangements. This is the funeral director's job – he or she will guide you through the planning of the service, complete the necessary paperwork, coordinate doctors, clergypersons, florists, newspaper announcements and other vendors to make your funeral experience as worry-free as possible. Ask about traditional and cremation options. A funeral can be as extravagant or as simple as you desire. To help avoid making choices at a time when your emotions are heightened, take a friend or two, or family members when meeting your funeral director.

C. Executing the estate. Be sure to get several copies of the death certificate from the funeral director. You will need copies for Federal pension authorities, insurance companies, pension plan managers and other interested parties. The estate will also have to pay off any creditors. You may want to consider using the services of a lawyer to assist with the estate administration.

D. Legal and tax considerations. Consult with a lawyer and/or accountant to discuss your spouse's estate and the filing of necessary tax documents.

You cannot finish the book of life, without closing its chapters. If you want to go on... then you have to leave the past as you turn the pages.

~ Unknown ~

CHAPTER 22
HOW TO HELP A FRIEND WHO IS GRIEVING

It's very difficult to help another person grieve unless you've been invited into the process. Until that invitation presents itself, you may feel helpless and there is little you can do to comfort your grieving companion. This feeling is natural and one that should not be dismissed. However, you can provide support by making yourself available. You can offer to help with practical things such as the provision of meals, housekeeping duties, caring for pets and even assisting with funeral details.

It's important to be a good listener. Encourage your friend to talk about their emotions and vent their frustrations. Take interest in the stories about his/her loved one's life and death. One suggestion – don't offer advice unless you have been asked to provide it, especially on topics you are unfamiliar with. Be patient, receptive, and encourage your friend to re-engage in their social activities, hobbies and interests.

Few people can cope with the pain of losing a loved one on their own. They need to talk about their loss and share their pain. This is a normal part of the healing process. However, if your friend's reactions are extreme, suggest professional help and assist them in taking this step.

Janice recently lost her husband Herb. He had not been well for the last 6 months and though the doctors were optimistic of Herb's recovery, Janice thought the worst. When Herb eventually died, Janice's immediate reaction was denial. Herb was always there and he will return. Janice then became angry not only at Herb for leaving her alone in retirement but also angry with herself for being reliant on him. He paid the bills, did the banking, dealt with their financial advisor, all the things Janice now has to do.

As part of Janice's grieving, she began thinking Herb would have lived longer if she only had made him see his doctor when he started to complain about his ailments. She also thought Herb would have survived longer if she was a 'better wife'. As weeks passed, Janice became resigned to Herb's passing and she began to pick up the pieces. Janice began paying the bills, closed out Herb's

---

bank account, met with the financial advisor, contacted a widow's support group and met with her religious leader about volunteering. Janice was moving on.

Throughout her grieving, Janice's friends, Alicia, Marcia and Joanne were with her every step of the way. They shared frequent phone calls, would meet for lunch, go on walks or just sit and talk. Her friends were Janice's anchors as she navigated through the stormy seas of grief.

CHAPTER 23
PETS IN RETIREMENT

Pets are lovable sources of companionship at any age. For many people, their pets truly are a part of the family and in some cases, these furry friends may have a higher ranking than other family members.

As you enter into retirement, your pet may be getting older with a life expectancy much shorter than your own. A common mistake made by retirees is immediately replacing "Muffin", "Mittens" or "Buster" without carefully evaluating the impact of the decision on their retirement plan. Consider a retiree who plans to travel, volunteer, and have hobbies outside of the home. They now have a new pet - possibly a kitten or a puppy - and are limited to out-of-home activities because of the need to care for the animal. As the pet grows, there may be a difficulty in leaving it for weeks at a time, especially when traveling or going on vacation.

More often than not, family and friends are reluctant to look after your pet, especially for long periods of time. The costs of kenneling can be high, not to mention the emotional aspects of leaving your pet in a strange place. If you plan on taking your pet with you when you travel, you may experience many hotels, inns and bed-and-breakfasts that do not allow them.

Part of Miranda and Nelson's retirement plan was to take a major trip once a year. Spice, their Irish setter was considered an important part of their family. When they traveled, their neighbors kindly took care of Spice as they also had a dog the same age and the animals were best of friends.

Just prior to Miranda and Nelson's retirement, their neighbor's dog died. Needless to say, everyone was saddened by the event, especially Spice who missed her long time companion. Much to Miranda and Nelson's surprise, their neighbors elected to not get another animal.

Two months later, Spice passed away from old age. Devastated and struggling to cope with their loss, Miranda and Nelson rushed out and bought a new dog

– an Australian Sheep dog named Tucker. For the next three months, Miranda and Nelson were housebound caring for their new pet. In this time Tucker became a beloved member of the family.

Comfortable with Tucker's development and training, Miranda and Nelson planned a trip to Greece. It was to be the trip of a lifetime. In the planning they assumed that their neighbors would care for Tucker while they were away. After finalizing plans and booking their tickets, they approached the neighbors to see if they would watch Tucker. The neighbors regrettably said 'no' as it would be too hard emotionally to have another dog in the house.

Prior to leaving for Greece, Tucker was placed in a kennel. Though they knew he would receive good care, Miranda and Nelson worried so much about Tucker's stay in a strange place that a lot of the enjoyment of Greece was lost and they regretted their decision to get another animal.

If you currently own a pet, there will come a time when you and your partner will face its passing. Prior to this happening, take time to discuss the advantages and disadvantages of obtaining another pet. Discuss your future retirement plans and determine if a pet is part of them. It is important to seriously consider the ramifications and commitment of owning another pet.

EXERCISE 35

Answer the following questions:

1. If our current pet dies, would we want another? Why or why not?

----

2. What problems may stem from us getting a pet at this stage of our lives?

_____

_____

_____

_____

3. What changes in our lives would make us consider getting a pet in the future if we don't currently have one now?

_____

_____

_____

_____

On the flip side, what happens to your pet if you are incapacitated, hospitalized or you die. As a pet owner, you should have a plan for the care of your pet.

1. Arranging for short-term pet care. Try to find a friend or relative who is willing to take care of your pet during any short-term periods brought on by illness or hospitalization. Leave notice in writing at home and with a neighbor or building management as to the friend or relative who is to be contacted. Be sure to arrange for access to your home. If you live in an apartment, consider leaving a key with the superintendent or neighbor. Consider giving your caregiver a key and written permission to enter the building and your apartment.

2. Arranging short-term care at a shelter or charitable organization. In the event of your hospitalization, provide the shelter or charitable organization with written instructions and permission for taking care of your pet. Give a copy to a neighbor, superintendent or building management. Don't forget to provide a key for access. It's also a good idea to leave written instructions with a relative or friend, who is to notify the shelter that has agreed to take care of your pet during your absence.

3. Designated caregivers. Find a friend or relative willing to take your pet and give it a good home if something should happen to you. This matter should be discussed in advance with your potential caregiver to make sure your animal will be cared for appropriately. The person who is to receive your pet as a result of a bequest in your will should understand that he or she becomes the pet's new owner and as such, has all the rights and responsibilities that go along with it. Ask your lawyer to include in your will the selected caregiver for your pet. It is a good idea to name alternate caregivers as well, in case the first-named person is unable or unwilling to take your pet when the time comes.

4. Providing funds for pet care. You may choose to leave a sum of money for your pet's designated caregiver along with the instruction that it be used for the care of the animal. Because your caregiver has no legal obligation to use the money for the purpose specified, it is important to select a caregiver you trust and who will be devoted to your pet. Be sure to leave only a reasonable amount of money as larger sums may prompt relatives to challenge your will. If this happens, a court may invalidate your bequest for pet care.

5. Designating a shelter. If you cannot find a friend or relative willing to take your pet, look for a charitable organization whose function is to care for or place, companion animals. A humane society or shelter might agree to accept your pet along with a cash bequest to cover expenses. Before selecting a shelter, find out what kind of care animals receive. Find out everything you can about the adoption procedure.

6. Providing for euthanasia if caregivers cannot be found. While you may feel it's important to protect your pet from mistreatment or a 'bad home', it is questionable whether a healthy pet's life should end by euthanasia when you die. Nevertheless, if you wish to provide for euthanasia, speak to your lawyer about specifying in your will that your pet is to be cared for by your executor or a friend for a specified period of time. During this time, ask that this person attempt to find a good home for your pet. If no home is found after reasonable effort and time, indicate that your pet may be euthanized. You can also write a letter to a friend or relative stating upon your death, your pet should be euthanized. A signed copy should be given to your friend or relative in advance, and another signed copy held with your will. Your letter is not legally binding and your friend or relative can choose whether or not to carry out your instructions.

As with all aspects of retirement, the ownership and care of pets requires a lot of discussion and planning. Don't rush into anything. Try to remove emotion from the decision process and think about the impact, both positive and negative, a pet will have on your retirement.

CHAPTER 24
MORE TIPS FOR A HAPPIER RETIREMENT

Happiness depends more on the inward disposition of mind than on outward circumstances.

~ Benjamin Franklin ~

A. How to Save Money

As a retiree and seasoned consumer, you need to continually ask yourself "How can I save money and still buy quality goods and services"? Though your expenses normally decrease overall when you retire, some expenses stay the same or increase, depending on your lifestyle choices. This is especially true if you are planning extensive travel or purchasing a 'big ticket' item such as a cottage or large boat.

The following are some proven ways to help cut costs:

Transportation

Airline Fares

1. Compare low-cost carriers with major airlines that fly to your chosen destination. Remember, the best fares may not be out of the airport closest to you.

2. You can often save money by including a Saturday evening stay-over or by purchasing your ticket at least 14 days in advance. Ask which days and times of the day have the lowest fares.

3. Even if you are using a travel agent, continue to check airline and Internet travel sites for special deals. When calling, always ask for the lowest fare to your destination.

New Cars

4. You can save thousands of dollars over the lifetime of a car by selecting a model that combines a low purchase price with low depreciation, good financing rates, low insurance premiums, excellent mileage, and low to average maintenance and repair costs. Ask your local librarian for new car guides that contain this information.

5. When you have identified the model and options you're interested in, you can save money by comparison shopping. Get price quotes from several dealers and let them know you are shopping around. You may also get a better price by taking a vehicle off the lot or one that is less popular in color.

Used Cars

6. Before buying a used car:

a. Compare the seller's price with the average retail price in a "bluebook" or other guide to car prices, which can be found at many local libraries.
b. Have a mechanic you trust check the car, especially if it is sold "as is."

7. Consider purchasing a car from an individual you know and trust. They are more likely than other sellers to charge a lower price and point out any problems with the car.

Gasoline

8. You can save hundreds of dollars per year by comparing prices at different stations, pumping gas yourself and using the lowest-octane called for in your owner's manual.

9. Pay attention to when price hikes happen at your local stations. Do they go up just before a weekend? If so, plan to buy gas when prices are traditionally lower, for example, Tuesdays and Wednesdays.

10. You can save over $100 a year on gas simply by keeping your engine tuned and tires inflated to their proper pressure. Check your tire pressure at least once a month.

Car Repairs

11. The most important step that you can take to save money on car repairs is to find a skilled, honest mechanic. Before needing repairs, look for a mechanic who is certified, well established and recommended by at least one person you know.

Insurance

Auto Insurance

12. You can save money by purchasing auto insurance from a licensed, low-price insurer. Call at least four of the lowest-priced, licensed insurers to learn what they would charge for the same coverage. Insurance brokers are another option that can help you find the lowest rates.

13. Talk to your agent or insurer about raising your deductibles on collision and comprehensive coverage to at least $500 or, if you have an older car, dropping this coverage altogether. Higher deductibles usually mean lower monthly payments.

14. Make sure you get age-related auto insurance discounts and credit for being a good, accident-free driver.

Homeowner/Renter Insurance

15. As with auto insurance, savings are realized when you shop around and purchase homeowner/renter insurance from a low-price, licensed insurer. Call at least four of the lowest-priced insurers to learn what they would charge. Again, using an insurance broker may help save time and money.

16. Make sure your insurance coverage is enough to replace your house and its contents.

Life Insurance

17. If you want only insurance protection, buy a term life insurance policy.

18. If you want to buy a whole life, universal life or other cash value policy, plan to hold the policy for at least 15 years. Canceling policies after only a few years can more than double your life insurance costs.

19. Consider having your children pay the premiums of insurance they will inherit.

Banking Credit

Checking Accounts and Debit Cards

20. You can save more than $100 a year in bank fees by selecting a free checking account or one with no minimum balance requirement. Request from your financial institution a complete list of fees that are charged on accounts, including ATM and debit card fees.

21. See if you can get a free or lower cost checking account through direct deposit or agreeing to ATM only use. Be aware of charges for using an ATM not associated with your financial institution.

22. Ask your bank manager about senior service charge discounts for checking and other bank related transactions.

Savings Plans

23. Before opening a savings account, use the telephone, newspaper and Internet to compare rates and fees offered by different financial institutions. Rates can vary greatly and choosing wisely can mean more money for you.

Credit Cards

24. Avoid late payment fees and possible interest rate increases on your credit cards by sending in your payment a week to ten days before the statement due date. Be sure to enquire at your bank about Authorized Monthly Due Date Payment services. Late payments on one card can increase fees and interest rates on other cards. If you are not the type to send in payments in advance, consider making payments on time, online.

25. Avoid interest charges by paying off your entire bill each month. If you are unable to pay off a large balance, pay as much as you can. Try to shift the remaining balance to a credit card or line of credit with a lower rate. You can find listings of credit card plans, rates, and terms on the Internet, in personal finance magazines and newspapers.

26. Be cautious of credit cards with rebates, cash back, travel rewards, and other perks as they may carry higher rates or fees.

Auto Loans

27. To save as much as several thousand dollars in finance charges, pay for the car in cash or make a large down payment. Always get the shortest-term loan possible, as this lowers your interest rate.

28. Make certain to get a rate quote (or pre-approved loan) from your bank or credit union before seeking dealer financing.

29. Make certain to consider the dollar difference between low-rate financing and a lower sale price. Remember that getting zero or low-rate financing from a dealer may make you ineligible for a manufacturer's rebate.

First Mortgage Loans

30. Although your monthly payment may be higher, you can save tens of thousands in interest charges by shopping for the shortest-term mortgage you can afford. For each $100,000 you borrow at a 7% annual percentage rate (APR), you will save more than $75,000 in interest on

a 15-year fixed rate mortgage than you would on a 30-year fixed rate mortgage.

31. You can save thousands in interest charges by shopping for the lowest-rate mortgage. On a 15-year $100,000 fixed-rate mortgage, lowering the APR from 7% to 6.5% can save you over $5,000 in interest. Check the Internet or your local newspaper for mortgage rate surveys. Then call several lenders for information about rates and fees. If you choose to use a mortgage broker, be sure he or she is an Accredited Mortgage Professional, and always compare their offers with those of direct lenders.

32. Be aware that the interest on most adjustable rate mortgages (ARMs) can vary a great deal over the life of the loan. An increase of several percentage points might raise monthly payments by hundreds of dollars. Ask the lender what the highest possible monthly payment might be.

Mortgage Refinancing

33. Consider refinancing your mortgage if you can get a new rate that is lower than your existing mortgage rate and plan to keep the new mortgage for several years. Mortgage professionals can calculate how much the new mortgage (including fees and closing costs) will be and whether, in the long run, it will cost less than your current mortgage.

Home Equity Loans

34. Be cautious of taking out home equity loans. The loans reduce or may even eliminate the equity built up in your home. Equity is the cash you would have if you sold your house and paid off the mortgage. If you are unable to make payments on home equity loans, you could lose your house.

35. Compare home equity loans offered by at least four reputable lending institutions. Consider the interest rate and the annual percentage rate (APR), which includes costs such as origination fees, mortgage insurance and other fees. Ask if the rate changes, and if so, how is it calculated and how frequently, as this will affect the amount of your monthly payments.

Housing

Home Purchase

36. You can often negotiate a lower sale price by employing a buyer broker who works for you, not the seller. If the buyer broker or the broker's firm also lists properties, there may be a conflict of interest. Ask if they are showing you a property that they have listed.

37. Do not purchase a house until a reputable home inspector that you select has carefully examined it. And don't rely on the seller's word or recommendation for an inspector. Knowing what is wrong or what expenses you are likely to incur with a home can be a point of negotiation and the difference between a happy home and a money pit.

Renting

38. Do not limit your rental-housing search to classified ads or referrals from friends and acquaintances. Select buildings where you would like to live and contact their building managers or owners to see if anything is available. Dealing directly may result in a lower rent as it saves advertising and showing costs.

39. Remember that signing a lease obligates you to making all monthly payments for the term of the agreement. Look at your finances, your retirement goals and the ability of subletting. If you are likely to move in the near future, a long-term lease may not be the best option.

Home Improvement

40. Home repairs often cost thousands of dollars and are the subject of frequent complaints. Having it fixed is not always the same as having it fixed properly and going cheap may end up costing you more in the long run if it's not done well. Select an established, licensed contractor who has submitted written, fixed-price bids for the work. Ask for references and check them out.

41. Be wary of contractors who are available to start immediately. The good ones are usually busy and more often than not, worth the wait.

42. Check to see if your area is serviced by one or more home service referral agencies designed to coordinate free quotations from independent contractors. Often times the agencies offer a double guarantee on work done – the contractor's guarantee and the agency's guarantee.

43. Do not sign or agree to any contract that requires full payment before satisfactory completion of the work.

Major Appliances

44. Go to a public library and consult Consumer Reports for information about specific appliance brands and models and how to evaluate them, including energy use. There are often great price and quality differences. Look for differences in warranty and the Energy Guide designation, which can save up to 50% in energy costs.

45. Once you've selected a specific brand and model, check the Internet and yellow pages to learn what stores carry the brand. Call at least four stores to compare prices and ask if that's the lowest price they can offer you. This comparison-shopping can save you as much as $100 or more. Don't be shy to ask about floor models as they are sometimes cheaper than warehoused units.

46. Enquire about home service rates and extended warranty programs. In some cases, it makes sense to purchase an extended warranty, which will more than pay for itself in the event a major repair is required after the initial warranty has expired.

Utilities

Heating and Cooling

47. A home energy audit can identify ways to save hundreds of dollars a year on home heating and air conditioning. Ask your electric or gas

utility if they audit homes for free or for a reasonable charge. If they do not, ask for a referral to a qualified professional.

48. Seek out local, provincial/state and federal grants for improving home efficiency in terms of environmental impact from reduced power and water consumption.

49. Consider enrolling in load management and off-hour rate programs offered by your electric utility. These may save you up to $100 a year in electricity costs. Call your electric utility for information about cost-saving programs.

Telephone Service

50. Once a year, review your phone bills for a three-month timeframe to see what local, long distance and international calls you are making. Check into different phone service providers to determine the cheapest calling plan that meets your needs.

You may also want to look into bundled packages that offer local and long distance calling and possibly other services such as mobile phones and Internet services at reduced rates.

51. Check your phone bill to see if you have optional calling features or additional services, such as inside wire maintenance, that you don't need. Each option you drop could save you $40 or more a year.

52. If you make very few long distance calls, avoid calling plans with monthly fees or minimums. Consider disconnecting the service altogether and use 'dial around' services such as 10-10 numbers or prepaid phone cards for your calls. When shopping for a dial around service, look for fees, call minimums and per minute rates. Treat prepaid cards as cash and find out if there is an expiration date.

53. If you use a cell phone, make sure your plan matches your typical calling pattern. Understand peak calling periods, area coverage, roaming and termination charges. Prepaid wireless plans tend to have

higher per minute rates and fees but may be a better option for occasional users.

54. Before making calls away from home, compare per minute rates and surcharges for cell phones, prepaid phone cards, and calling card plans to find how to save the most money. A little bit here and there adds up to a lot at the end of the year.

55. Dial your long distance calls directly. Using an operator to place the call can cost you up to $10 extra. To save money on 411 or information calls, look the number up on the Internet or in the directory.

Food Purchased at the Market

56. You can save hundreds of dollars a year by shopping at lower-priced food stores. Convenience stores often have the highest prices so the more organized you are the more you will save.

57. You will spend less on food if you shop with a list, take advantage of sales and purchase basic ingredients rather than pre-packaged components or ready-made items.

58. Don't shop for groceries when you're hungry. With all those options, impulse buys are almost impossible to resist.

59. You can save hundreds annually by comparing price-per-ounce or other unit prices on shelf labels. Stock up on items with low per-unit costs.

Prescription Drugs

60. Brand name drugs are usually more expensive than their generic counterparts. Ask your doctor or pharmacist if a less expensive generic or over-the-counter alternative is available.

61. Pharmacies may charge widely different prices for the same medicine, so be sure to call several before having a prescription filled.

When taking a drug for a long time, consider using mail-order pharmacies, which often charge lower prices.

Funeral Arrangements

62. Plan ahead and make your wishes known for your funeral, memorial or burial arrangements. Putting it in writing could save your family or estate a lot of unnecessary expense.

63. For information about inexpensive options, contact a local Funeral Consumer Alliance or memorial society, usually listed in the Business Classified Section in the phone book under funeral services.

64. Before selecting a funeral home, call several and ask for prices. Visit the funeral homes to obtain an itemized price list.

65. Consider prepaying for your funeral arrangements. Not only does prepaying relieve your family members from the financial burden, prepayment allows you to comparison shop and often locks in prices. However, it is a large expense and there is no guarantee that the funeral home will still be in business when the services are required.

Discounts and Freebies

66. Visit the many websites offering discounts and free stuff. Companies and organizations offer substantial discounts and freebies for many things such as: computers, clothing, household articles, health and beauty aids, laundry products, candy, ring tones, magazines, car rentals, hotel accommodations, games, travel insurance, just to name a few. A word of caution, watch out for fraudulent websites. If in doubt, contact the offering companies regarding their participating websites.

67. When attending a concert or movie, going to a restaurant, getting a haircut or pedicure or any other event or occasion, ask for the senior's discount. You will be amazed how many organizations offer from 5 to 50% off the regular price in appreciation of their senior patrons and customers.

68. When making a purchase on just about anything, inquire about a senior's discount. Whether it is a book, a car rental or travel insurance – ask!

Tipping

69. Tipping was once reserved almost exclusively for waiters, waitresses, hairdressers, cabbies and bellhops. Unfortunately, the practice has now expanded to include fast-food restaurants and coffee shops. To save your money ignore the tip jar. You are not obligated to tip when no real 'service' has been provided.

Loyalty Programs

70. If you are a member of a travel miles or hotel points program you can swap, buy, earn, share or redeem miles or points in more than 25 of the world's leading loyalty programs. You can track the balance of all your accounts from one location. Points International manages your accounts as if they were a stock portfolio. You can also take advantage of hundreds of redemption options. For information, go to www.points.com.

EXERCISE 36

List ten ways you plan to save money when you retire.

1. _____

2. _____

3. _____

4. _____

5. _____

6. _____

7. _____

8. _____

9. _____

10. _____

B. Tips for living on a budget:

The following are several tips on how to live on a budget:

• **Don't dump unaccounted-for expense dollars into 'miscellaneous'.** The more specific your tracking, the easier it is to find those extras that are the least painful to cut. Do you dine out at breakfast or lunch on workdays? Brown bagging a few of those meals can mean real savings. Just $2 a day means an extra $730.00 dollars at the end of the year; save $5 a day and you'll have $1,825.

• **Pay yourself first.** When you pay your bills, set aside some money to deposit into your savings account. Paying yourself $50 each month becomes $600 a year in savings.

• **Consolidate your debts.** You may be able to take care of several small loans or credit card bills with one larger loan at a lower interest rate. You can also use some of your savings to pay off those debts if the interest charges are higher than the interest earned from your savings.

• **Reduce your insurance premiums.** Accept a higher deductible or cancel collision coverage on an older vehicle you may not repair if in an accident.

• **Leave room in your plan for rewards.** Don't eliminate all the 'fun' expenses or you'll lose your motivation to stick to your cash plan.

Instead, try to tone down or cut back on some forms of entertainment or recreation. For example, play one round of golf a week, rather than two; rent one movie rather than two; substitute get-togethers with friends at home rather than going to a restaurant.

• **Keep paying paid-off debts.** After you make your final payment on your car or mortgage, keep writing those monthly checks but this time, put the money in your savings account.

EXERCISE 37

These are the changes I will make to financially assist me in obtaining my retirement vision and goals:

_____

_____

_____

_____

_____

_____

_____

_____

_____

_____

_____

CHAPTER 25
WAYS TO REDUCE YOUR CHANCES OF FRAUD OR BURGLARY

A. Protecting Yourself from Fraud

A broad definition of fraud is 'deliberate misrepresentation, which causes another person to suffer damages, usually monetary losses'. Many fraud cases involve complicated financial transactions by persons with specialized knowledge and criminal intent.

An unscrupulous investment broker may present his clients with an opportunity to purchase shares in, let's say, precious metals repositories. His status as a professional investor gives him credibility, which can lead to a justified believability among potential clients. Those who believe the opportunity to be legitimate contribute substantial amounts of money and receive authentic-looking bonds in return. If the investment broker knew that no such repositories existed and still received payments for worthless bonds, then the victims may sue him for fraud.

Unfortunately fraud is not easily proven in a court of law. One of the most important things to prove is a deliberate misrepresentation of the facts. Did the seller know beforehand that the product was defective, or the investment was worthless?

The element of fraud that tends to stymie successful prosecution is the obligation to investigate. It falls on potential investors or customers to fully investigate a proposal before any money changes hands. Failure to take appropriate measures at the time of the proposal can seriously weaken a fraud case in the courtroom later.

The accused can claim the alleged victim had every opportunity to discover the potential for fraud and failed to investigate the matter thoroughly. Once a party enters into a legally binding contract, remorse over the terms of the deal is not the same as fraud.

If you suspect you are a victim of fraud, consult a legal professional and collect all tangible evidence of damages.

Unfortunately, in today's world there are many scams and frauds taking place – from charity misrepresentations and accounting frauds to computer scams, just to name a few. Extreme caution is to be exercised! If you are approached in person, by telephone or e-mail to invest, send money, donate, or learn you have won a trip or prize, or anything else that sounds too good to be true, it probably is. Be cautious and think twice about the information being provided. Don't let yourself become a victim! If you have any doubts, just say "No!"

Do

- Check your account statements promptly and immediately report any transactions you don't recognize
- Destroy all receipts before discarding since some may have your card number printed on them
- Guard your card – don't use it as collateral or give your card number to someone on the phone, unless you initiated the call for a purchase
- Shred all personal and financial information – such as bills, bank statements, ATM receipts and credit card offers – before you throw them away
- Keep your personal documentation (i.e. birth certificate, social insurance card) and your bank and credit card records in a secure place
- Call the post office immediately if you are not receiving your mail. To get the personal information needed to use your identity, a thief can forge your signature and have your mail forwarded
- Be aware of your surroundings when entering your Personal Information Number (PIN) at an ATM
- Limit the number of credit cards and other personal information that you carry in your wallet or purse
- Report lost or stolen credit cards immediately
- Decide whether you need inactive card accounts. Even when not being used, these accounts appear on your credit report, which is

accessible to thieves. If you have applied for a credit card and have not received the card in a timely manner, immediately notify the appropriate financial institution

- Monitor the expiration dates on your credit cards. Contact the issuer if the replacement card is not received prior to your credit card's expiration date
- Sign all new credit cards upon receipt
- Review your credit reports annually
- Use passwords on your credit cards, bank accounts and phone cards. Avoid using the obvious passwords – your mother's maiden name, your birth date or phone number

Don't

- Volunteer any personal information when you use your credit card
- Give your social insurance number, credit card number or any bank account details over the phone unless you initiated the call and know the business that you are dealing with is reputable
- Leave receipts at ATMs, bank counters or unattended gasoline pumps
- Leave envelopes containing your credit card payments or checks in your home mailbox for postal carrier pickup (i.e. rural mail boxes)
- Record your social insurance number or passwords on paper and store them in your wallet or purse. Memorize your numbers and passwords
- Disclose bank account numbers, credit card account numbers or other personal financial data on any website or online service location, unless you receive a secured authentication key from your provider
- For further information on frauds and scams, visit www.wisegeek.com/what.

B. Travel Scams

As you are approaching retirement, you and your spouse may be thinking of traveling. If so, be aware of scammers and thieves. Here are some tips for keeping your money in your wallet and not someone else's.

1. Have you won a free trip in a contest you didn't enter? Ignore the call. According the Better Business Bureau, travel-related fraud costs consumers over $10 billion a year. It is best to deal with a travel agent or major on-line company.

2. Ask for the price before you order. At restaurants, a common trick is to overcharge tourists. Before ordering your meal, check the menu and prices. Have a good understanding of the local currency and learn a few phrases in the local language. This gives the impression you are familiar with the area and more difficult to dupe.

3. When ordering or traveling in a cab, exercise caution. Arrange your cab transportation through a reliable source rather than hailing one on the street. Ensure the cab is in good condition. Prior to your trip, consult a map before heading out to get a feel of the streets and when in the cab, pay attention to where you are going. Avoid cabs that already have occupants and request your driver not to stop to pick up other passengers. If you suspect something is wrong, get out of the cab.

4. When in a foreign place, research and learn how to tell the real police from the fake. Know what a local police uniform looks like. If approached by an 'officer', ask to see his or her badge. Note the name and number on the badge. Call the local police station to verify the person is in fact a police officer.

5. Find out about known local scams before traveling to your destination. In Spain and the Netherlands, it's lottery scams. In the Philippines and Laos there are credit card scams.

6. Know how to get advice and help. Have a plan and know whom to contact for help. Do not rely on a stranger but rather your embassy, the local police or your travel service and insurance provider. Have the respective telephone numbers written down before leaving home.

C. Protecting Your Identity

Unfortunately, in today's world there are unscrupulous people who are on the lookout for personal information that can be used to commit fraud or other crimes in the victim's name. The best way to minimize your chances of becoming a victim is to be aware of the various ways thieves collect personal information. Though thieves keep inventing new and elaborate schemes to obtain your personal information, here are the most common:

1. Dumpster Diving: ID thieves search trash and recycling bins for personal information such as credit card statements, purchase receipts and income tax papers. The best way to protect yourself is to use a crosscut paper shredder to destroy all personal and financial information that is no longer needed.

2. Shoulder Surfing: Confidential information such as your PIN number or password can be stolen by looking over your shoulder when using a public computer, laptop, PDA or other devices in common places. As a precaution, be aware who is near you when entering personal or confidential information. Get into the habit of using your hand to shield your PIN number even when no one is around as thieves sometimes use hidden cameras.

3. Use of Spyware: Spyware is software that is secretly installed on home or public computers to collect personal information. Spyware can be installed in various ways: by visiting infected websites, downloading software or applications from the Internet such as screensavers, games, etc. Your best defense is to install anti-virus and anti-spyware software as well as a personal firewall on your home computer. Don't use public computers for online banking or other financial activities. Never let a website or software memorize your password.

4. Phishing: Thieves use unsolicited e-mails and fraudulent websites that closely resemble legitimate business sites. Their goal is to trick you into revealing personal or financial information such as usernames, passwords, account numbers and SINs. To protect your information, never click on a link inside an e-mail that asks you to connect to and/or verify your personal information. If you receive unsolicited e-mail claiming you have "won a prize" or "we need to confirm your banking account numbers, passwords, etc." flag it as junk and immediately delete the e-mail.

5. Vishing: Similar to phishing, thieves call and try to trick you into divulging personal and financial information over the phone. When in doubt about a call from a bank or other institution, contact the main offices of the facility represented. Most institutions will never ask for passwords or PIN numbers over the phone and would rather you visit them in person at your local branch.

6. Mail Theft: Thieves can steal your personal information from your mailbox. Monitor the timing of when your credit cards will be renewed and when bills are supposed to arrive. If they don't arrive when expected, notify the issuer immediately.

7. Shopping Online: Identification thieves can steal your personal information by tricking you into using fake websites to purchase products or services. Make sure you shop only at websites that you know are reputable and trustworthy. Look for a small lock displayed in your browser that lets you know the site is secure.

EXERCISE 38

There are many ways to protect yourself from fraud. What will you do?

Ways I Plan to Protect Myself from Fraud

_____

_____

_____

_____

_____

_____

_____

D. Protecting Yourself from Burglary

In North America, about 20% of property crime (fraud, possession of stolen property, theft and motor-vehicle theft) is done via breaking and entering.

Source: National Crime Victimization Survey - property crime trends 1973-2005, US Dept. of Justice - Office of Justice Programs, Bureau of Justice Statistics, September 10, 2006

Though there is no one alarm system that will make your home completely secure, the installation of a home monitoring system will help deter burglars from breaking in. The most basic home alarm system is just that – an alarm. If some one tries to enter your home through a window or door while the system is armed, a high-pitched siren goes off alerting you and the entire neighborhood. More sophisticated systems include interior motion detectors, noise sensors, breaking glass detectors and security cameras.

Self-installed security hardware can be purchased at a cost of appropriately $10-25 per window or door. Motion detectors cost about $30 and whole house packages are roughly $250. You may also consider installing a monitored alarm system. Equipment and installation charges range from free - providing you sign up for a multi-year contract, to over of $1,000 depending on your needs. Monthly monitoring fees range from about $25 to $50.

Whether you install a home alarm system or not, the following steps will reduce the likelihood of your home being burglarized:

• Don't leave a spare key under a mat, on top of the doorframe or under a plant. Burglars know all the usual hiding places.
• Lock your front door when you're in the house or working in the backyard and make sure all windows and doors are locked every time you leave.
• Don't hang your car keys in a visible spot by the door. Many burglars break into homes just to get the keys to bypass car alarms on many high-end vehicles.
• Don't keep valuables in plain sight such as a jewelry box on top of the dresser. Store them in a safe or safety deposit box.

- Join Neighborhood Watch and/or work with your neighbors to keep an eye on each other's houses.
- When on vacation, have a neighbor or friend collect your mail and newspapers and get them to shovel the snow or mow the lawn as required.
- Take photos and video and make a detailed list of valuables, including serial numbers to provide to the police and your insurance company in the event of a break-in.

CHAPTER 26
LIVING RETIREMENT TO ITS FULLEST!

When looking back at life, many retirees have regrets about what they did not accomplish. Some may take responsibility for their failures but often people blame the obstacles others placed in their way. They have dozens of excuses for not achieving their goals and ended up settling for second best. Unfortunately, these same retirees enter retirement unprepared. They end up wasting precious time and energy - wishing things were different. They struggle through their retirement without a vision and plan and in the end, ask themselves, "Is this all there is?" They cheat themselves out of the best years of their lives.

As you enter the second longest phase of your life, you have the opportunity to 'get it right' the first time. You have 10, 15, 20, maybe even 25 years or more in front of you, in which you can realize your hopes and dreams. To make this happen, you need to know what you want and create a plan that will get you there.

If you have read this far in the book, been honest with yourself and completed the exercises to the best of your ability, then you have a plan. You know what you want and should have a good idea on how to get it. Always remember that your plan is an active, living document. Wants, needs and desires change and so may your plan. Keep it close and review it often.

If you don't know where you are going, you will probably end up somewhere else.

~ Laurence J. Peter ~

This book is intended to assist you on the journey down the retirement road. Hopefully you have gained new information and insight and the exercises have prompted your thinking about who you want to be in retirement and the actions you need to take to make it happen.

As the final assist in your quest, the following are actions to making the next phase of your life - the BEST!

- **Seek and find the new role called 'retirement'.** Speak with people who are successful in their retirement. Find a mentor. Read articles and books about retirement. Attend seminars and lectures on the subject and become fully informed. Contact retirement agencies such as the Canadian Association of Retired Persons (www.carp.ca) or the American Association of Retired Persons (www.aarp.org) for information.

- **Maintain your personal independence.** Continue to handle your financial affairs and make decisions that affect you for as long as possible. Remember, it is important to stay in control.

- **Make a major effort to maintain your best possible state of health and resist complaining about your ailments.** Continue to take a personal pride in your appearance, both clothed and unclothed.

- **Explore your options and interests.** Consider your options and choose whether you want to continue with your profession or trade, volunteer or develop creative endeavors. Keep your mind and body active and your spirits high.

- **Take action to make a positive contribution to the lives of others.** Ask yourself, "What will my legacy be when I die?" "How will I be remembered?" and "Did I make a positive impact on the lives of others?"

- **Create and maintain good relationships with others.** Sustain your social circle and let people in your circle know they are important to you. Keep reaching out to meet new people and make new friends.

- **Continue to learn.** Read, return to school, take self-improvement and development courses. Keep developing your skills and abilities.

- **Remain a positive force within the community as long as possible.** Speak up, take action when necessary and become a matriarch or patriarch within your family circle.

- **Maintain and build your sense of humor.** Laugh and enjoy where you are in life, see yourself in perspective, and the positive side of things.

- **Handle setbacks with grace and strength.** When illness, loss of a spouse, or problems with children arise, talk to others and get assistance to help you cope. Develop an action plan aimed at getting through the setback as quickly as possible.

- **Have a personal dignity in all that you do.** Keep increasing your vitality and interest in life.

EXERCISE 39

Review your retirement vision. Keeping in mind the information presented in this book and your completed exercises, what refinements are needed to accomplish your retirement plans and achieve your retirement goals?

Notes:

_____

_____

_____

_____

_____

_____

_____

_____

DEAR READER,

Thank you for your interest in retirement planning. I wish you all the best in living your retirement dream!

At the start of this book, I invited you to take a journey to explore various aspects of retirement and construct a retirement plan tailored to meeting your needs and matching your vision. You were asked to complete a number of exercises designed to prompt thought and inquiry. You were encouraged to share your ideas and approaches so you could learn from the experiences of others, as they would learn from you. I sincerely hope your journey was thought provoking and rewarding.

In an effort to share your discoveries with others, I encourage you to drop me a note indicating how your retirement plan is unfolding. Please let me know about your experiences, successes and challenges you face as you progress down the retirement road. Your insights and words of wisdom will be made available to others who follow in your footsteps.

I will leave you with these words of encouragement:

Cherish your vision and your dreams as they are the children of your soul; the blueprints of your ultimate achievements.
~ Napoleon Hill ~

Yours sincerely,

Richard Atkinson
RAMGT@rogers.com

ABOUT THE AUTHOR

Richard Atkinson, President of RA Retirement Advisors, is an expert in pre-retirement planning. Known for his practical, interactive and results oriented workshops, Richard has helped people throughout North America plan for a successful and fulfilling retirement.

With over 35 years experience as a human resources management specialist, Richard has worked as both an internal and external HR consultant in the manufacturing, oil and gas, mining, health and social services sectors. His consulting services have also been contracted to municipal and provincial levels of government.

In addition to a Master of Business Administration from York University in Toronto and a Bachelor of Commerce – Honors degree from the University of British Columbia in Vancouver, Richard holds the Ontario Society of Training and Development *(now the Canadian Society of Training and Development)* Advanced Level Certificate of Achievement.

Richard is a volunteer advisor for the Canadian Executive Service Organization (CESO) and a volunteer consultant for Toronto's Management Advisory Service (MAS).

Now retired, Richard is happily married to Christine and they are the proud parents of four daughters and the grandparents to seven grandchildren. Together they are fulfilling their individual and shared retirement dreams in Toronto, Ontario, Canada.

REFERENCES

Dr. Robert Anthony, "Total Self-Confidence", Berkley Books, (1979)

Bank of Montreal, "What Identity Thieves Do Not Want You to Know", (Feb. 2008)

"The Benefits of Journaling, How to Get Started", www.stressabout.com.

Richard N. Bolles and John E. Nelson, "What Color is Your Parachute, For Retirement", Ten Speed Press, (2007)

Dianna Booker, "Communicate with Confidence", McGraw-Hill Inc. (1994)

Allen Britnell, "Sounding the Alarm", www.improvinghome.ca.

Bureau of Business Practice Editorial Staff, "Complete Retirement Workshop, Your Guide to Planning a Secure & Rewarding Future", Bureau of Business Practice, (1993)

Canadian Mental Health Association, "Grieving", www.cmha.ca.

Elwood N. Chapman, "Comfort Zones, A Practical Guide for Retirement Planning", Reid Publishing, (1985)

Stephen Cherniske, "The Metabolic Plan", Random House, (1993)

Nathan Cobb, "Mindset, You Are What You think". Check-Up, Issue 38, (2008)

Sherry Cooper, "The New Retirement", Penguin Group, (2008)

Stephen R. Covey, "The 7 Habits of Highly Effective People", Simon & Schuster, (1989)

Merrill E. Douglas and Donna N. Douglass, "Manage Your Time, Manage Your Work, Manage Yourself", American Management Association, (1980)

John W. Drakeford, "Growing Old – Feeling Young", Ballantine Books, (1985)

Ken Dychtwald, "Age Wave", Jeremy P. Tarcher, Inc. (1989)

50plus, "Renovate for Live-In Parents", www.50plus.com.

David Foot, "Boom, Bust & Echo", Macfarlane, Walter & Ross, (1996)

Debbie Ford, "The Secret of the Shadow", HarperCollins, (2002)

Lillian Glass, "Toxic People", St. Martin's Griffin, (1995)

Michael Gordon, "Old Enough to Feel Better, A Medical Guide for Seniors", Fleet Books, (1981)

Michael Gordon, "An Ounce of Prevention, The Canadian Guide to a Healthy and Successful Retirement", Prentice-Hall Canada, (1984)

John Grobe, "How Much Income Do You Need in Retirement, It Depends", Fedsmith.com, Wednesday, July 18, 2007

Thomas Harris, "I'm OK – You're OK", Avon Books, (1973)

Robert J. Havighurst, "Developmental Tasks", Freudian Slip. www.freudianslip.co.uk

"Hiring a Home Care Worker", www.careguideathome.com.

Elizabeth Holtzman, "Emotional Aspects of Retirement". www.umass.edu

James A. Lawson, "Canadian Retirement Planner", Bessborough Publishing, (1984)

Alec Mackenzie, "The Time Trap", American Management Association, (1990)

New York Bar Association, "Providing for Your Pets",
www.nycbar.org.

RBC Financial Planning, "Retirement Planning",
www.rbcfinancialplanning.com.

Marsha Sinetar, "Do What You Love, The Money Will Follow", Dell
Publishing, (1987)

M. Irene Sharkey-Orgnero, "Procrastination, Five Tips to Get You
Going", Check-Up, Issue 38, (2008)

Social Security, USA, "Retirement Benefits", SSA Publication No. 05-
10035, (January, 2008)

"Spirituality and Aging", www.cas.umkc.edu/casww/sa

Statistics Canada, 2006 Census, The Daily, Tuesday, (July 17/07)

Statistics Canada, Population Projections, 65 Years and Older,
Catalogue no. 91-520-XIE, (September, 2007)

Statistics Canada, Time Spent on Leisure by Adults Aged 55 and
Older, 2005, Catalogue no. 89-622-XIE, (September, 2007)

Marika and Howard Stone, "Too Young to Retire", Penguin Group,
(2004)

US Census Bureau News, August 14, 2008 (CB08-123)

US Department of Health and Human Services, Publication No.
2007-1232

US Department of Justice – Office of Justice Programs, Bureau of
Justice Statistics, September 10, 2006

Matt Weinstein, "Managing to Have Fun", Simon & Schuster, (1996)

"Why Does Your Metabolic Rate Drop as You Age?" www.thefactsaboutfitness.com.

Blossom T. Wigdor, "Planning your Retirement", Grosvenor House Press, (1985)

Maryanne Vandervelde, "Retirement for Two", Bantam Books, (2004)

INDEX

Do you know someone who is retiring soon?
Maybe someone who is just thinking about it?
Better yet, someone who should be?

Don't Just Retire – Live it, Love it!
makes a great gift for family, friends and colleagues

Get additional copies today by filling out and faxing the order form below to (416) 282-4260 or going online to **www.dontjustretire.com** and we will rush your order out to you!

- ORDER FORM -

Hey Rick!

Please send me _____ copies of "Don't Just Retire - *Live it, Love it!*" at 24.95 each (plus S&H).

Please ship to:

Name: _____

Address: _____

City: _____

Prov/State: _____ Postal/Zip Code: _____

Email address: _____

Phone: _____

☐ MC   ☐ VISA   ☐ AMEX

Card #: _____ Expiry: _____